Getting Hip

Recovery From A Total Hip Replacement

By

Sigrid Macdonald

authorHOUSE

1663 LIBERTY DRIVE, SUITE 200
BLOOMINGTON, INDIANA 47403
(800) 839-8640
www.authorhouse.com

First published by AuthorHouse 10/18/04

ISBN: 1-4184-7838-5 (e)
ISBN: 1-4184-7837-7 (sc)

Library of Congress Control Number: 2004094594

Printed in the United States of America
Bloomington, Indiana

This book is printed on acid-free paper.

ADVANCED PRAISE

"Although our body is a finely tuned machine with expected surgical outcomes, this practical and reader friendly book reinforces we each have a unique medical presentation. After reading this, not only will you have a comprehensive understanding of all aspects of Total Hip Replacements, you will have permission to vary from the expected norms and accept your own rate of recovery."

Wendy Rogers, Physiotherapist (BPT)

"Hip replacements have granted a new lease on life to countless folks. If you are considering this surgery for yourself, you need this first-hand comprehensive report from someone who has done the research for you. Ms. Macdonald provides a wealth of information on the challenges facing hip replacement patients and the resources they require dealing with this experience.

As a nurse, and possibly a prospective future candidate, I found everything one could wish to know and more in *GETTING HIP*. This lay person's account of the modern experience of hip replacement surgery is a must for any professional wanting to understand the bewildering landscape of hip replacements in North America. Sigrid details the range of possibilities available to patients, from choosing a doctor to deciding on a specific type of implant, as well as making plans for aftercare. Ms. Macdonald has covered it all in a very warm and entertaining manner."

C. Soubliere R.N. BSc PHN

"*GETTING HIP* takes the reader through the experience of a total hip replacement, from the first problem signs to total recovery. It gives a clear, witty, intelligent and thoroughly readable account of the whole process, and contains valuable information for patients, caregivers and professionals. Macdonald has researched the subject comprehensively, and gives excellent advice for anyone contemplating this major operation. Various surgical methods and devices are also discussed, as well as the future of hip replacement in general. All anyone needs to know about this procedure is here."

Una Holmes, Fellow Veteran of a Total Hip Replacement

DEDICATION

This book is dedicated to my mother,
Muriel, for her endless years
of devotion, emotional support and
self-sacrifice.

ACKNOWLEDGEMENTS

I am deeply grateful to Dr. Joseph Pizzurro, my first orthopedic surgeon, who saved my life and my left hip after it had been fractured and dislocated in a car accident. In addition, I would like to thank the doctors and nurses at Valley Hospital in Ridgewood, New Jersey, who took care of me and made it possible for me to walk normally once again. This includes Dr. Mark Sherman, Dr. David Lipson, and Dr. Gisela Ucko. I also appreciated the kindness of Dr. David Myers of Oakland, New Jersey, who oversaw my orthopedic care for many years.

Dr. Patrick Murnaghan performed my total hip replacement at the Civic Campus of the Ottawa Hospital. I will be forever indebted to him and the incredible staff on the orthopedic ward and in the short-term rehabilitation unit of the hospital, as well as to his efficient and compassionate assistant, Linda Carvill. I am much obliged to Tracy Silverson and the staff at River Park convalescent home for looking after me following my surgery. And I will never forget the help that I received from one of River Park's residents, Carl Killeen, and for the excellent care from my family doctor, Edward Ragan, and his dedicated assistant, Judy Denney.

My physiotherapists and occupational therapists were exceptional: they include Jackie Manning, Janice Wood, Wendy Rogers, Barbara Dickson and Jennifer Clark. Jill Castonguay, my mental health nurse, offered me emotional support during a difficult time, as did Marjorie Swarthout, the Chaplain at the Ottawa Hospital. I am grateful for a number of services that I received from Community Care Access Centre and the Visiting Homemakers Association, especially for the cheerful help from my personal support worker, Sarah Hamilton. I sincerely appreciated the flexibility of Nepean Seniors, who drove me to medical appointments, although I am not a senior. Bruce Connolly and Tom Clark, two drivers from the seniors organization, were sweet and entertained me with their offbeat sense of humor. And I would like to particularly thank Alex Ranger, the wonderful manager of The Putting Edge golf course in Nepean, for teaching me how to play mini golf and for not laughing at me when I used my reacher after surgery to pick up the balls; Alex and his staff (Matt, Mark and Kati) are the reason that mini golf has become my favorite game post-op.

There are simply no words to express the gratitude that I feel towards my family members starting with my mother, Muriel, who has been my greatest supporter, and serves as the foundation in life from which I draw all of my strength. My sister, Kristin, has been a warm and sympathetic listener throughout the years and my brother, Brooke, and his wife, Alicia, have been generous to me and concerned about my well-being. Christopher, my 15-year-old nephew, spent hours showing me how to create a web site, which acted as the precursor to this book. And Oliver, my 17-year-old nephew, designed the dazzling cover for GETTING HIP. Last but not least, I would like to thank my dear belated father, Hugh, for his love and devotion and for teaching me never to give up!

My friends were a godsend during the difficult time before and after surgery. Hubert and Estelle McKinley, Una Holmes, Suzanne Pepin, Cathie Soubliere, Beryl Arnold, S. J. Markman and Warren Wilson offered precious moral support and practical assistance. Long-distance friends like Margaret Agne, Ed Remington, Robert Ferry, Debbie Merlin, Joyce Milgaard, Blair Roger and Jill Greene were equally supportive.

I am beholden to the ten individuals who took time from their busy schedules to be interviewed by me: Thelma Lubkin, Arlette Hill, Gillian Smith, Ralph Stevens, Lucy Hoover, Gerard Kelly, John Parke, Suzanne Carlos and Michael Bentley. One of my interviewees did not wish to be named in the book so I gave him the pseudonym of Edward Marshall. Ranny Welton went to the trouble of filling out my detailed questionnaire but I was unable to use him in my interview section because, at that point, I was looking for people over the age of 65. However, I have alluded to his experience in my introduction.

Janet Hanson, Clinical Manager of Orthopaedics[1] at the Ottawa Hospital, kindly gave me permission to use several illustrations from the hospital's "Patient Information: Total Hip Replacement" booklet. Therese B. Murphy, from the department of Research & Scientific Affairs at the American Academy of Orthopaedic Surgeons,

---

[1] This book has been written using Standard Edited American English. Therefore, I have spelled the word orthopedics with an "e" except in direct quotes by individuals or in reference to certain organizations that use the Canadian or British spelling of the word, which is "orthopaedics."

sacrificed her time to answer my many questions. And Linda May-Bowser, founder of the Internet *Totally Hip Support Group*, shared her knowledge and expertise, and allowed me to use an x-ray that was taken of her left hip following revision surgery.

Lastly, my friend Anita Flegg, who wrote her first book last year, inspired this book. *GETTING HIP* would not exist at all without the superb guidance and encouragement of my book coach, Dr. Serena Williamson. I am extremely grateful to Wendy Rogers, Una Holmes, Cathie Soubliere and Mark Pendergrast for reading parts of my manuscript and offering important tips for improvement. Special thanks to Cheryl Driskell for her invaluable feedback on my material, and to Suzanne Pepin for hours of meticulous editing. Finally, I sincerely appreciated the help that I received from Amber Olmstead, Teri Watkins and Kyiesha Isiah at AuthorHouse publishing company.

TABLE OF CONTENTS

INTRODUCTION

Every year, almost 400,000 North Americans undergo joint replacement surgery. Arthritic hips, knees, shoulders and occasionally, ankles are replaced with metal and plastic implants. Total hip replacements (THRs) constitute approximately half of these surgeries, allowing people who would otherwise be completely disabled by pain to resume full and active lives.

We are in the miraculous era of the Internet, the DVD, the CD player, the Cell Phone and the Palm Pilot. It is easy to take these technological advances for granted and to forget that they were all developed and made accessible within the last twenty years. Likewise, the first successful total hip replacement was not performed until the early 1960s. Fifty years ago, those who were afflicted by severe arthritis would have suffered relentless pain with no hope of effective treatment. In many instances, they would have spent the rest of their days in a wheelchair. Dr. Seth Leopold, of the Orthopedics and Sports Medicine Department at the University of Washington, considers the total hip replacement to be the most important operation developed in the 20th century, in terms of the amount of human suffering that it has relieved.

In April of 2003, I was one of 17,500 Canadians who required a total hip replacement. Many people have swift recoveries from hip surgery. The books that I read indicated that most people were able to dispense with their crutches about six to eight weeks after the operation, and that three months postoperatively, they felt relatively normal. This was not my experience nor was such a textbook recovery shared by all of the people that I interviewed.

I had a significant degree of pain and swelling in my leg that lingered for months after my THR. Although I was only 50 years old, which is young in the world of hip replacements, I needed to use a walker for more than ten weeks. I spent an additional eight weeks on a cane. Instead of feeling well three months after the surgery, my hip did not feel anywhere near normal until five or six months postoperatively. At first, I thought there was something wrong with me. I felt inadequate and worried that something had gone wrong with my operation, because it took so long to regain my muscular strength and the ability to walk again comfortably. Then I created a web site about my experience and began talking to other people who had had the surgery. I discovered that I was not alone. Not everyone had a speedy and painless recovery, although most people experienced considerably less pain than I did and regained mobility much faster; but several of those individuals required multiple joint replacements later on.

Some of my suffering was needless. I made many mistakes, which I would like to share with prospective hip patients, so that they can benefit from my errors. Unlike other surgeries, people cannot sit back, relax and let time heal the wound following hip surgery. They need to be active participants in their own rehabilitation. Information is power. If you are considering a hip replacement, the more you learn about the operation beforehand, the better off you will be.

This book is geared towards people who are wondering if they need a total hip replacement and to those who are waiting for hip surgery. It is also written for individuals who have already had their hips replaced, especially if they are under the age of 65. There is a strong likelihood that they will have to have additional hip surgery down the road since the average lifespan of an artificial joint is only 10 to 15 years.

GETTING HIP may serve as a useful tool for friends and relatives of people who are undergoing joint replacements. I offer a great deal of information about how I decided to have the surgery, what is involved in the preoperative exam, and the mechanics and history of the operation itself. In addition, I provide a detailed description of my own rehabilitation, from the time of the surgery to six months postoperatively, as well as advice on how to take care of a new artificial hip and a final chapter on the future of hip replacements.

Each patient is unique. An arthritic hip may be the only health issue facing some individuals whereas others, like me, may have additional medical problems. One person might have an extensive social support network, a large family or a supportive spouse, whereas another person might live alone and have very little assistance. One patient may recover quickly and effortlessly with minimal pain and another may experience a delayed recovery with quite a bit of discomfort. 55-year-old Ranny Welton of Mexico, Missouri drove himself to work one week after his hip replacement.

He used a walker in the hospital, went home with a cane, and was walking without any assistive devices two weeks later! But 73-year-old Suzanne Carlos of Ottawa, Ontario spent months on a cane following her surgery. Age is not always the determining factor in recovery, either. After my surgery, the orthopedic nurses told me that sometimes patients in their eighties or nineties resume walking right away, yet someone in their forties or fifties may take much longer.

My own recovery did not occur until somewhere around the fifth or sixth month after surgery. The timetable for other people's recoveries varies. I have included interviews with ten people who have had hip surgery. Nine of these individuals had total hip replacements. One had a procedure called hip resurfacing, which results in fewer restrictions than total hip surgery, since the hip is reshaped rather than replaced. Most of the interviewees reside in the United States but two are living in Canada. One is in the United Kingdom and another is in Denmark. They range in age from 43 years old to 70 years young at the time of their THR, and most are quite satisfied with the results of their surgery.

Some people may think that the title of my book, *GETTING HIP*, is too facetious or lighthearted for such a serious subject. I have deliberately chosen an upbeat title because I believe that humor is an important component of the recovery process. There is nothing funny about hip replacements but I did have some amusing experiences during my rehabilitation. I have tried to laugh about these occasions and to share my comical moments, as well as my difficulties and frustrations.

I hope that this book will be read by members of the medical profession and by the staff that treat total hip patients, such as nurses, physiotherapists, occupational therapists, visiting home nurses, counselors, and home care workers. Often, in their day-to-day jobs, medical personnel are only able to spend brief amounts of time with their patients. They cannot grasp the extent to which a patient's life has been affected by the deterioration of an arthritic joint, and the difficulty that is involved in going through total hip surgery.

GETTING HIP is also directed at health care policy makers. The accident that caused my hip injury took place in New Jersey, which makes this an American story. But my surgery took place in Ontario so this is also a Canadian story. We have universal health care in Canada. When it works properly, our Medicare system is fantastic because everyone is insured. Health coverage is a right in this country, not a privilege. However, our health care system is overburdened and underfunded. Consequently, there are long waiting lists to get in to see a specialist and even longer lists for surgery. I had to wait 18 months for my operation. This was in addition to the 18 months that it took to decide that I was going to have the joint replaced. That translated into three completely lost years for me.

The baby boomers are turning 50. As the population ages, the incidence of arthritis and the subsequent need for total hip replacements will increase. The Canadian Orthopaedic Association and the Canadian Arthritis Society have joined forces to warn the public of "a crisis in joint replacement surgery." Both organizations claim that there is not enough manpower to perform the surgeries and that people are waiting far too long. We need more orthopedic surgeons in Canada and we must learn to treat our nurses and physiotherapists with more respect and remuneration, so that these crucial medical people do not continue to emigrate south of the border. Surgeons need better access to operating rooms. We need more hospital beds so that orthopedists have a place to put their patients once they have scheduled operations. New advances in joint surgery are exciting, but they will be of limited usefulness if the Canadian national health care system cannot make this routine operation available to people in a timely fashion.

Waiting lists may not be an issue for Americans but insurance coverage is often a problem. 43 million Americans lack health insurance, according to CNN's medical authority, Dr. Sanjay Gupta. The uninsured tend to receive catastrophic care in the emergency room. They are less likely to receive preventative treatment. Medicaid, Medicare and Health Maintenance Organizations cover millions of other Americans. HMOs are notorious for creating delays in the approval of medical procedures, including hip replacement surgeries. Chris Warner is the owner of Panther Enterprises, a physician recruiting service in Long Beach, California. He says,

"The morass of government programs and private insurance plans is bewildering, extremely convoluted, complex and very expensive: some say at a cost of two hundred billion dollars a year. Physician's offices are rampant with cascades of forms, paper, regulations, codes, manuals, phone calls, hair wringing and teeth gnashing as a direct result of this third party oversight, due to spending constraints by individuals and employers. As a result the basic fabric of our health care system is in grave jeopardy." Thus, Americans, Canadians and Britons, who also have a public health care system, all experience some type of frustration with access to joint replacement surgery.

Lastly, this book may be of interest to the dedicated people who campaign against drunk driving. I needed hip surgery before I turned 50 because I fractured and dislocated the joint at the age of 28 when I was hit and badly injured by a drunk driver. My hip became arthritic, eventually wore out and needed to be replaced. For many years, I was a member of Mothers Against Drunk Drivers and Remove Intoxicated Drivers. I appeared on three television shows about drunk driving including *20/20, 60 Minutes* in Australia, and a Manhattan cable TV show entitled "Alcohol Abuse." According to Mothers Against Drunk Drivers, in 2002, 17,419 people were killed in the U.S. in crashes involving alcohol, representing 41 percent of the 42,815 people killed in all traffic accidents. Fortunately, lobbying efforts have paid off and alcohol-related fatalities have decreased significantly since my accident in 1981. Injuries have also declined but still number about 500,000 each year in the United States alone. Even one serious injury can alter a person's life forever.

Finally, I hope that I can convey my sense of awe for the science of joint replacement and my gratitude that I was born at a time when such impressive technology could relieve my suffering.

1

My Hip Injury

I love summer. Like most captives of Northern Ontario, I eagerly anticipate the end of spring so that I can dispense with my ski jacket, boots, and headband in favor of shorts, T-shirts, and running shoes. I like to sit outside on my front steps listening to the robins sing, watching the neighbors, and basking in the warmth of the sun.

I spent a lot of time sitting on my front steps during the summer of 2000 until I became aware of a nagging pain in my left hip. I've always had to be careful about sitting in certain positions for long periods of time since I fractured and dislocated my hip in an auto accident in 1981. I was visiting my parents in New Jersey when I was hit by a drunk driver and nearly killed. I sustained multiple injuries including a concussion, whiplash, a punctured and collapsed lung, several broken ribs, and a number of broken bones, such as fractures of my hip, pelvis, wrist, arm, knee, and lower leg bones. After three weeks in intensive care, I was moved to the orthopedic ward. I developed Post-Traumatic Stress Disorder and suffered from panic attacks, recurrent nightmares about car crashes, and flashbacks for many years. I was 28 years old at the time and as the band R.E.M. so succinctly put it, the accident was the end of my world, as I knew it.

Initially, my hip was set with a closed reduction, meaning that my orthopedic surgeon put my hip back into place manually after it dislodged. However, the nurses in the hospital were busy and did not always answer call bells promptly. One day I was dying for a bedpan and decided that I simply could not wait 20 minutes for a nurse to appear, so I cleverly bent down towards a small cabinet by my bed to get the pan. I was very pleased with myself until I began to experience horrific pain. Sure enough, I had dislocated my hip again by twisting my body forward. This time the solution was not so easy!

My surgeon, whom I affectionately but brazenly called "Joey," told me that in order to repair my hip, he would have to put me in K-wire traction. This involved the surgeon and his team drilling a hole straight through my already broken knee to insert a wire from one side of the knee to the other. One Saturday morning, he appeared at my bedside looking like a carpenter with a full set of nasty looking tools wrapped around his waist. I had been given a local anesthetic but it did not put a dent in the searing pain I experienced. Nor could it assuage the extreme anxiety and distress that was prompted by watching my orthopedist drill a hole through my knee. When the brutal procedure finally ended, the doctor put 25 pounds of weight at the bottom of the wire, and placed me in a position that is called Trendelenberg.

Anyone who has been in this uncomfortable position knows that Trendelenberg was probably devised by the Nazis. It required me to lie backwards in bed with my legs tilted up towards the ceiling for five long weeks. I was only allowed to sit up for meals, sponge baths, and other ablutions. Like the ghost of Jacob Marley tormented by his chains, I felt the wire inside my knee every time I switched positions. This caused great discomfort. To say that I was relieved when the wire was removed would have been a gross understatement.

I was not a very good patient. Before the accident, I had completed one and a half years towards a two-year Masters in Social Work at the University of Toronto. I was enamored with Toronto and content with my life. I enjoyed my studies and commanded a certain degree of respect as a graduate student. That ended abruptly with the accident when I found myself bedridden, in constant pain, and sleep deprived.

During the three months that I spent in the hospital, I had eleven roommates and every one of them snored! I began to desperately crave sleep, which caused tension between my doctor and me. There were no private rooms on the orthopedic floor so I requested to be moved to a medical ward. My surgeon was opposed to this; he knew that I would not receive proper care on another floor since the nurses on the orthopedic ward were specially trained to deal with my particular injuries. In retrospect, I understand that the doctor was protecting me by keeping me on orthopedics, but at the time,

I was unhappy about the chronic exhaustion that resulted from my sleepless state.

My injuries had rendered me completely dependent on other people. It was frustrating and embarrassing to continually ask others for assistance. I struggled against a sense of helplessness and anger as was evidenced by insisting on getting my own bedpan, and brashly calling the surgeon by his first name.

When I was discharged from the hospital, I went to stay with my parents in order to learn to walk again. Five days a week, a private ambulance took me for intensive physiotherapy throughout the winter and spring. On a daily basis, I did a number of exercises to strengthen the quadricep and hamstring muscles in my leg. I also worked on flexing and rotating my hip joint. Eventually, I progressed to lifting weights with my injured leg and working out on a stationary bicycle.

I was non-weight bearing on crutches for six months before I graduated to a cane. A year after the accident, I was walking without any assistive devices but I had a significant degree of pain in both my left hip and knee. When I got a second opinion on my hip in 1982, the surgeon looked at my x-ray and immediately suggested that I have the joint fused. Hip fusion, otherwise known as arthrodesis, eliminates pain in the hip joint but the joint no longer has a wide range of motion. This can present problems with certain activities like getting in and out of a car and may significantly strain the back and knees. I had no such desire to restrict my movements and continued diligently with my exercise program, which eventually paid off.

I spent many years lobbying against drunk driving after I discovered that the man who hit me had a blood-alcohol level of .23, which was more than twice the legal limit. The driver was doing 70 miles per hour in a 30 mile per hour zone and hit me head on. At the age of 37, he had a record of driving infractions that went back 19 years. His license had been suspended and revoked a number of times and he had been caught driving without a license. My "accident" was not an accident after all; the man was a reckless driver and a self-described alcoholic. Our collision could easily have been prevented if the State had stepped in earlier to permanently revoke his driving privileges. Even after my accident, the man's license was only suspended for one year before he was able to drive again, and he was never charged with causing me bodily harm. He received the same sentence for hurting me that he would have received for running a red light.

It took time for me to forgive the man who had hit me. As a member of Remove Intoxicated Drivers, I was offered an opportunity to appear on *20/20* and to be interviewed by John Stossel. The show, entitled "It's Not My Fault," was broadcast as a Christmas special on December 26, 1985. The driver also appeared on the program along with the owner of the local restaurant bar that served him. I successfully sued both the drunk driver and the bar under the Dram Shop Law, which held third parties responsible for serving too much alcohol to drivers.

Appearing on *20/20* and on *60 Minutes* in Australia allowed me to meet the drunk driver in person and to forgive him for turning my life upside down. The man was contrite, remorseful, and apologetic. He had stopped drinking immediately after the accident and thanked me for his sobriety. He told me that he started out every day of his life with a prayer for my health and recovery. The bar owner did not take any responsibility for the accident. He was indignant and felt victimized by my lawsuit against his restaurant. I understood the owner's position. I have always been ambivalent about the host liability act. How can a bartender tell who has had too much to drink in a crowded nightclub? Ordinarily, this would be difficult, but in my case, the bar that I sued was a small family restaurant that only served alcohol to ten or twelve people at a time. The man who hit me drank there frequently and the restaurant knew him. With a blood-alcohol level of .23, surely the bartender would have noticed that this regular customer was intoxicated.

By 1983, I had settled my legal disputes out of court. However, my health problems lingered on. The pain in my hip and knee had decreased to a tolerable level but the fractures had caused osteoarthritis in both joints. Before the accident, I had lived in Toronto without a car. I loved to walk and would walk four to five miles a day. I also enjoyed ice skating and sitting cross-legged on the floor. After the accident, I could not risk falling on ice nor could I rotate my hip into that yoga-like position in order to sit cross-legged. Like most people with arthritis, I began to learn the frustration of living with some degree of pain and limitation.

In addition to the soreness in my hip, I developed chondromalacia, a condition that causes damage to the kneecap and results in pain and swelling. And I had torn ligaments and cartilage in my knee, which could not be repaired surgically. I could no longer kneel since putting weight on my knee caused acute discomfort. Nonetheless, I walked well and did not have a limp. I could walk one mile a day and that was adequate for my new suburban lifestyle. For many years, the pain in my joints was manageable and did not interfere appreciably with my life, unlike the fibromyalgia and Chronic Fatigue Syndrome that resulted from the accident. Muscle pain and exhaustion became my daily companions. I was never able to return to work or to finish graduate school in Toronto, despite several attempts to do so. Over the next decade and a half, I worked as a volunteer at various women's centers, was active in politics, wrote freelance articles, and acted as a research assistant at a local university whenever my health permitted.

THE DECLINE OF THE JOINT

During the summer of 2000, my hip joint began to bother me again. At first, I thought that I had simply put the hip into a bad position by spending so much time sitting on the front steps with both knees raised higher than my hips. I began to sit on a lawn chair but this did not relieve my pain, so my doctor referred me to physiotherapy. In September, my therapist and I began working on different exercises for my hip. One involved me lying on my back and bending my left knee towards my chest in order to improve my hip flexion. After doing this exercise for about two weeks, I put my back out and was unable to walk for three or four days. At the time, I did not realize how interconnected the hip and the back were. This was the first of many episodes where my back would completely collapse on me as a result of the degenerative arthritis in my hip. After my back healed several weeks later, I timidly resumed the exercises. Within days, I was unable to stand on my left leg due to sharp, stabbing pain in my hip. It was so acute that I spent three and a half hours being investigated in the emergency room of a local hospital.

5

The doctor examined my x-ray and exclaimed, "Looks like you need a hip replacement!" "No way!" I replied. I was convinced that he was wrong. My hip had served me well for almost 20 years. Even though I was told at the time of the accident that I would need to have the joint replaced eventually, I did not believe that the time had come. I was 47 years old. I was too young for a hip replacement! The joint had only started to bother me within the last few months and I thought that it had been sprained by the physiotherapy exercises. I was certain that it would recover.

Despite the severe deterioration evident on the x-ray of my hip taken in the hospital, and the fact that I could hardly bear any weight at all on my leg, I refused to accept the fact that I needed the hip replaced. As the saying goes, "Denial is more than a river in Egypt!" Disbelief and denial were my first reactions to the diagnosis and I held on to them for at least a year after the episode in the emergency room. The average life span of an artificial hip is only 10 to 15 years. I was afraid that if I had the procedure done in my forties, I would need to have at least two more joint replacements during my lifetime. However, I accepted the hospital's painkillers and had them refer me to a rheumatologist and a surgeon, despite my skepticism about the diagnosis.

The appointment with the rheumatologist was arranged quickly. I saw her within five or six days of my emergency room visit. She concurred with the emergency room doctor that the joint needed to be replaced. I was given a prescription for Celebrex, an anti-inflammatory drug, which made me sick to my stomach. We had to bypass the first line of treatment with the NSAIDs (nonsteroidal anti-inflammatory drugs) like aspirin or Advil because reliance on the latter had given me fourth degree ulcers.

Initially, I dealt with the hip pain by being as inactive as I could. The less I moved, the less my hip hurt. I started doing all of my cooking sitting down on a chair. I would drag a chair from the kitchen table over to the stove or to the refrigerator, using it as my own portable wheelchair, because I could not stand up to cook for even five minutes. When I went out with my friends, I would have them drop me right at the door of a restaurant, so that I would only have to limp in on my cane for 20 to 30 feet. I would sit in the car outside of the grocery store, feeling guilty and useless while my mother or my friends did my shopping.

CONSULTING WITH THE FIRST SURGEON

I braced myself for a similar diagnosis from the orthopedic surgeon, whom I was finally able to see that November. The doctor surprised me. He was loquacious, which was unusual for a surgeon. He spent at least 30 to 40 minutes talking to me and asked me all kinds of questions. He then began to describe a doom and gloom scenario; he told lurid tales about everything that could go wrong during the hip surgery. I could get a blood clot that could travel to my lungs or my brain, and provoke a stroke or kill me. The new hip could dislocate. I could get an infection that would necessitate re-operating, with a chance that my hip joint would be so damaged that I would have to spend the rest of my life in a nursing home, confined to a wheelchair. I could have a heart attack on the operating table or the surgeon might accidentally break my leg during surgery. I found this conversation to be unduly frightening, and decided to research the likelihood of any of these events actually occurring to me.

POSSIBLE SURGICAL COMPLICATIONS

According to the American Academy of Orthopaedic Surgeons, more than 170,000 total hip replacements are performed each year in the United States. In the United Kingdom, patients receive more than 50,000 artificial hips annually. The Canadian Orthopaedic Foundation states that more than 37,500 hip and knee replacements are undertaken in Canada each year and the number is rising annually due to an aging population. Almost half of those are total hip replacements (THRs) and most of them are required as a result of advanced osteoarthritis, says Dr. Robert Bourne, professor of orthopedic surgery at the University of Western Ontario. Bourne is the director of the Canadian Joint Replacement Registry (CJRR,) a project set up in the summer of 2000 to monitor and track the number of hip and knee replacements in Canada. "About 2.5 percent of the entire population or 1 in 40 Canadians will have a hip or knee replacement at some point," Bourne claims.

Worldwide, approximately 500,000 hip replacements, also known as arthroplasties, are conducted every year. For the most part, joint replacements are very successful and dramatically improve the quality of life for the recipients. Like any major surgery, there are risks. There is a risk of blood clot or infection following a total hip replacement but every precaution is taken to reduce the incidence of these complications. Patients are given large doses of intravenous antibiotics to prevent infection, operating rooms are especially designed to filter out bacteria, and sterile techniques are employed. If the prospective hip patient has any kind of infection, from bacteria in the urinary tract to the common cold, the surgery will not be performed. Most sources agree that the chance of contracting an infection following total hip replacement is somewhere around 1 percent.

Deep vein thrombosis (DVT) is the most common cardiovascular complication following a hip replacement. This is when blood clots form in the deep veins of the legs. The American Academy of Orthopaedic Surgeons states that 80 percent of orthopedic surgical patients would be likely to develop DVT, and 10 percent would be likely to develop a pulmonary embolism if preventive treatment were not provided. Preventive treatment consists of providing postoperative patients with anticoagulants and anti-embolism stockings, called TEDs. Even with these prophylactic measures, deep vein thrombosis and subsequent pulmonary embolism remain the most common cause for emergency readmission and death following joint replacement, the American Academy notes.

Certain people are at greater risk of developing a thrombosis. People who smoke, are overweight, are on estrogen or who have had a history of previous DVTs are more likely to develop a blood clot following hip surgery. Other people are genetically predisposed towards blood clots. Studies show that the use of a spinal rather than a general anesthesia may reduce the likelihood of a DVT by up to 50 percent.

3.6 percent of patients will experience a potentially fatal pulmonary embolism, according to Dr. Richard Villar, British orthopedic surgeon, and author of the book *Hip Replacement: a Patient's Guide to Surgery and Recovery*. That is why Coumadin, an anticoagulant, is routinely given to patients along with shots of heparin to make their blood thinner. Many doctors require hip patients to wear TED stockings, which reduce swelling. They are encouraged to get up within 24 to 48 hours of the surgery to get their circulation moving in order to avoid a blood clot.

Villar states that the risk of death from a total hip replacement or THR is about 1 percent, but the development of these complications depends on many factors, such as age, general state of health, and surgical expertise. If patients are over the age of 80, Villar claims that up to 20 percent of them will experience some form of postoperative problems. The risk of developing complications also rises significantly during hip replacement revisions. Problems are less likely to occur during the primary hip replacement.

Another potential risk of the total hip replacement is that one leg may be longer than the other following surgery. This happened to Ryle Miller, a retired engineer from Vermont, who had both a hip and a knee replaced. He was able to correct this unfortunate problem by building up the soles of his shoes. The book *Hip and Knee Replacement: a Patient's Guide* was co-authored by Miller and his orthopedic surgeon, Geoffrey McCullen. Miller was a veteran who was traveling through Europe in 1971 when his knee went out on him. At the age of 48, he was diagnosed with rheumatoid arthritis and went through a grueling series of gold shots and treatment with cortisone pills. Miller attained dramatic but short-lived relief with this regimen. After he discontinued the gold shots, his old symptoms of fatigue, painful muscles, and morning stiffness returned. He struggled with these until 1987 when he twisted his left knee snowshoeing. Miller then tried injections of cortisone, oral anti-inflammatories, and a knee brace. He even had a knee arthroscopy to prevent the need for joint replacement, to no avail.

An arthroscopy is a way of looking inside the knee or hip joint via fiber optics to assess the status of the joint. Sometimes, pieces of tissue, bone or bits of cartilage and ligaments can be repaired via arthroscopy. But it is not a valuable technique for treating severe arthritis because of the extensive joint deterioration involved. Miller did not find relief from pain until he received a total knee replacement in March of 1989. He felt reasonably well afterwards until he was diagnosed with Parkinson's disease. Parkinson's interfered with Miller's balance and made him unsteady on his feet; he took a fall while working in his backyard. He fell 30 feet, broke his pelvis and injured his hip, necessitating a total hip replacement and a 17-day stay in the hospital. Miller had more than his share of joint replacements, which is not uncommon for someone whose joints have been damaged by rheumatoid arthritis.

In terms of my own hip dilemma, I knew that the surgeon I saw had to protect himself legally. He would not have wanted me to sue him if I developed an infection or a blood clot, and had not been forewarned. I am sure that he was a good doctor but I did not feel reassured by his manner. Since I was already opposed to the operation, the surgeon's alarmism strengthened my fear and denial. Although he did offer to operate on me, he did so reluctantly. It was clear that he wanted me to spend several more years on painkillers and a cane before I considered a THR.

PREVENTING HIP SURGERY

That was fine with me. About six weeks after my trip to the emergency room, the screaming pain began to abate and I became a bit more mobile. I began to read everything I could on ways to prevent hip surgery. I had already tried physiotherapy, ice packs, moist heat, aspirin cream, ultrasound, glucosamine and chondroitin sulfate, and Celebrex. Carrying additional weight is a strain on an arthritic joint. Luckily, I am on the slim side so I did not have to lose weight to take pressure off the injured joint. I had been living in shock absorbing running shoes for some time, which reduced the impact of walking on the hip joint. And I had severely curtailed my weight bearing activities, such as walking, climbing stairs, and standing for any length of time. I decided to forego massage, chiropractic, homeopathy, and acupuncture because they were too expensive and had not worked for me in the past. Lastly, my arthritis was much too advanced for an arthroscopy.

Instead, I started swimming twice a week and following the program set out by Dr. Robert Klapper and Lynda Huey in their excellent book *Heal your Hips: How to Prevent Hip Surgery — and What to Do if You Need It*. This instructive manual advocates a program of specific exercises to strengthen and restore mobility to the hip joint. The exercises are to be done ten minutes per day on land and ten minutes per day in the swimming pool. Klapper warns against repeated use of cortisone shots, which can damage the joint. This is an informative and sensible book that may work well for people whose joints have not deteriorated significantly. All of my hopes for the aquatic cure vanished one day when I got stuck at the pool because I could no longer get my socks and shoes back on after swimming. I had no choice but to ask the woman next to me for help. I began to understand why James Dean said, "Live fast, die young, and leave a good-looking corpse." Yes, and preferably one whose joints functioned! If this was middle age, I needed to investigate cryogenics.

The pool episode left me feeling discouraged but it helped to break my cycle of denial. There was no doubt in my mind after the incident that I was going to need the joint replaced. The question became when I would have it done and with whom. Although I had booked surgery with the first surgeon I saw, I decided that I would not be comfortable with him operating on me, so I cancelled my surgical date and began to look for another orthopod.

GETTING A SECOND OPINION

Specialists are busy people. They do not have vast amounts of time to spend with patients. However, I wanted to find a doctor who would provide me with a reasonable amount of time, answer my questions, and alleviate my concerns about the effect of the surgery on my other health problems. I am a consumer of medicine and have every right to shop around for a good doctor.

When I was young, I was full of admiration for physicians. My late father was a medical doctor. Those were the days of Marcus Welby, M.D. and Ben Casey. Doctors were held in such high regard that they were seen as almost mythical creatures. There is an old joke about a Jewish mother whose son was elected President of the United States. A friend turned to the woman during the inaugural ceremony and said, "Oh, but you must be so proud!" The mother replied, "Yes, but you should see his brother. *He's* a doctor!"

Nowadays, doctors are not necessarily held in high esteem. In my 23 years as a career patient since the car accident, I have dealt with dozens of doctors and have seen an abundance of their shortcomings. Many were abrupt, arrogant, and presumptuous. Others were well intentioned but quick to jump to diagnostic conclusions without taking a proper history. They did not listen well.

Specialists, in particular, were notorious for their haste and lack of empathy.

A 2002 study conducted by Fuschia Sirois and Mary Gick of Carleton University in Ottawa, Ontario examined the beliefs and motivations of patients who sought out alternative medicine practitioners. Sirois and Gick concluded that the individuals who were most likely to choose an alternative or complementary practitioner were people who had multiple health problems, greater awareness of health behaviors and predictably, dissatisfaction with conventional medicine. Unpublished findings from the same study indicated that many patients who abandoned traditional medicine complained that their doctors had failed to take the time to listen to them. In order to make a proper diagnosis, it is crucial for doctors to hear their patients. Some participants in this research project compared their medical visits to being on "a conveyor belt," or to being moved through the office "like cattle," an experience that I can certainly relate to.

Most of the doctors that I saw during the 1980s and 1990s did not spend enough time with me. As a result, they misdiagnosed my problems. Physicians routinely dismissed my multiplicity of physical complaints as nothing more than depression. I believe that there is a bias against patients with chronic health problems. Often, the size of my medical file alone would lead a doctor to conclude that I was a hypochondriac. In addition, although I do not see sexism lurking behind every dark corner, I do suspect that my health problems would have been treated more seriously if I had been male.

In fact, a study from the Toronto Rehab Center indicates that women in high socioeconomic brackets have less access to joint replacement surgery than do men of a similar income bracket. Toronto Rehab is an organization that specializes in rehabilitating people who have had joint replacements. This research, published by Dr. Gillian Hawker and co-developed by Dr. Jack Williams, revealed that people communicate differently with their doctors according to their gender. Women are the greatest consumers of health care. The 8th annual ACNielsen study of consumer health-related attitudes and behavior found that women are more likely than men to visit a doctor, consult with a pharmacist, and take vitamins and/or minerals. Men, on the other hand, are more likely to "tough it out" when they experience medical symptoms. Women are more verbal about their bodily ailments whereas men are apt to be more stoical. If women complain more often than men do, doctors may perceive women's health problems as being less serious than men's physical challenges.

It took many years for me to assemble a team of doctors whom I felt were bright, compassionate and on target with my health. Now I have a group of physicians whom I like, admire, and respect. My family doctor is a kindhearted and intelligent soul, who always takes the time to listen to me and to be thorough. I wanted to find an orthopedic surgeon with similar qualities. Having a hip replacement is not like having a gallbladder removed. I will remain in close contact with my surgeon for some time and will continue to see him or her many years after the operation. I wanted someone who was highly skilled and would give me the facts about the operation without terrifying me.

A friend of my mother's had just had her hip replaced by a prominent surgeon at a local hospital. I called her and asked a number of questions about her doctor. I spoke to other people who had had hip replacements and asked how they felt about their surgeons. I decided to book an appointment with the surgeon who had operated on my mother's friend to see if I liked him. A doctor at my neighborhood clinic made the referral and I waited several months for a consultation.

The doctor was bright, warm and had a twinkle in his Irish eyes. After viewing my x-rays, he immediately agreed to do a THR and apologized for the length of his waiting list, which was 12 months long. He informed me of all of the potential risks of the surgery but unlike the earlier surgeon, this man did not overwhelm me. He assured me that the procedure was routine and generally successful — some studies estimate that the probability of patient satisfaction following a primary total hip replacement is as high as 90 percent — and he did not seem to have a problem operating on someone who was under the age of 50. I was impressed with his reputation and his bedside manner. The surgeon had performed numerous hip replacements and had a specially designated orthopedic floor in his hospital, as well as a short-term rehabilitation unit. I felt comfortable with him and knew that I could work with him.

During our interview, I told the surgeon how much my hip was affecting my daily activities and my mood. I added that hip pain and restrictions on my range of motion in the joint were preventing me from having intercourse. The surgeon seemed surprised by this and assured me that most of his patients were able to maintain a reasonable sex life. I was hard-pressed to imagine just who these gymnasts could be. Were these the same little people in his waiting room who could not walk a city block, were bent over their walkers and canes, and were popping Advils just to get through the day? Was there a Kama Sutra that I had yet to discover for the arthritically challenged? Sex was only one of many activities that were no longer possible for me as my hip continued to deteriorate. Walking, standing, bending, and lying down were all extremely painful. Shopping, cooking and doing laundry were very difficult; recreational pursuits were impossible. The more pain that I experienced, the more I limited my activities, which resulted in boredom and depression.

2

Waiting for Surgery

WAIT IS A FOUR LETTER WORD

I put my name on the surgeon's list and went home to wait. Instead of waiting 12 months as I had expected, I waited 18 months. Why is the waiting list for joint replacements so long in Canada? Millions of people suffer from arthritis and disabling pain and their numbers are increasing as the population ages. Secondly, there is a shortage of orthopedic surgeons in this country. Many have retired, died or become part of the "brain drain" that has immigrated to the United States. The Canadian Orthopaedic Foundation states that there are only 900 orthopedic surgeons in Canada today and that nurses, anesthesiologists, physiotherapists, and occupational therapists are also in short supply. Budget cutbacks and inadequate staffing often necessitate the closing of orthopedic wards or cancellation of surgeries. Doctors have difficulty booking time in operating rooms and finding available beds for their patients. Surgical cancellations serve to further increase the backlog of patients who are waiting for joint surgery.

The Fraser Institute, an independent public policy organization, says that the median waiting times for replacement of the hip, knee, ankle, or shoulder after an appointment with a specialist were as follows in 2003:

Saskatchewan: 72 weeks
British Columbia: 52 weeks
Alberta: 32 weeks
Quebec: 24.5 weeks
Manitoba: 26 weeks
Ontario: 24 weeks
Prince Edward Island: 29.5 weeks
Nova Scotia: 52 weeks
New Brunswick: 16 weeks
Newfoundland: 16 weeks

This does not count the additional 13.3 weeks that the average Canadian must wait in order to see a doctor for orthopedic surgery after receiving a referral from a general practitioner. The Canadian Orthopaedic Association and The Arthritis Society have joined together to raise public awareness about the problem of waiting lists. Dr. George Prize, of the British Columbia Arthritis Society, claims that more than two million baby boomers will be diagnosed with arthritis in the next 15 years. "During this time, the number of people with arthritis will increase even faster than the rate of the population increases," he declares. "If you think it will be costly to look after these people properly, just wait until you see how much it will cost not to look after them."

Delays in surgery are expensive. The Institute of Health Economics in Canada estimates that bone and joint problems like arthritis cost approximately $18 billion a year in lost productivity. This is not to mention the incalculable social and psychological toll on patients and their families. The Canadian Press states that there are currently about 20,000 Canadians waiting for hip or knee replacement surgery, and studies have shown that the longer people wait for surgery, the less successful the operation may be.

Secondary problems may arise, according to physiotherapist Wendy Rogers. "Surgical options are only considered with advanced deterioration in the hip joint. Compensatory changes occur in the muscles, fascia and ligaments altering the biomechanics of the whole body by affecting all the joints of the lower limb, pelvis and spine. Muscle imbalances and postural adaptation occur resulting in an asymmetrical gait. Once the hip is surgically replaced and the natural alignment restored, the myofascial changes remain... the result is shortened painful structures to be rehabilitated postoperatively. Consequently, early intervention to prevent secondary problems makes sense before irreversible changes occur."

HMOs — HEDGING MY OBLIGATIONS

American patients may experience long delays with their HMOs. It may be difficult for them to obtain a referral to an appropriate specialist, to receive approval for the hip replacement itself and to get a date for surgery. Some patients decide to take matters into their own hands and become their own advocates. They spend an inordinate amount of time making telephone calls or writing letters urging their HMOs to authorize procedures.

Other unfortunates may have their requests for hip surgery denied altogether. 72 million people in the United States are covered by HMOs, according to an article in the Associated Press by Anne Gearan. In June of 2004, two people took their HMOs all the way to the Supreme Court, arguing that the insurance carriers refused to pay for treatments that were prescribed by their doctors. The claims were rejected in a unanimous decision by the court, which did not want to set a precedent for multimillion dollar lawsuits against Health Maintenance Organizations. This was a setback for patient's rights. "By reserving the right to decide what is — and what is not — medically necessary, managed care plans can now practice medicine without a license, and without the same accountability that physicians face every day," the American Medical Association said afterward.

Some HMOs deny coverage altogether to people who have had joint replacements. My fantasy about moving to Florida was shattered when I contacted Blue Cross and Blue Shield after my hip surgery. They told me that I was not eligible for coverage under their HMO plan because I had metal parts inside my body. Other private health insurance companies in Florida offered me basic coverage at $350 per month, which would insure me for medical problems that I would probably never develop. But the firms made it clear that they would put a waiver on both my hip and knee because these joints may need to be replaced in the future. Thus, in order to leave the bitter Ontario winters behind and enjoy life in the Sunshine State, I would have to pay $4,200 annually for catastrophic health coverage. This would not include deductibles and co-payments and more importantly, I would be forced to assume the entire cost of two joint replacements if I needed them in the future. It is common for health insurance companies and HMOs to exclude coverage for pre-existing conditions; this problem can affect anyone with an artificial prosthesis who decides to move, switch jobs, retire or who becomes self-employed or unemployed.

During the interminable wait for my own surgery, my hip began to affect every aspect of my existence, from my relationships to my finances to my emotional state. Some weeks, I was completely crippled. Very short distances appeared daunting, such as walking from the front of the supermarket to the back of the milk aisle. I began parking illegally in front of the library because I could not walk up to the building from the handicapped parking space with my cane. I could not even walk to my mailbox, which was about 300 feet from my front door! On one occasion when I was desperate to get to the movies, I called the theater beforehand to ask them if they would let me in through the back door, since I could not walk from the parking lot to the ticket counter at the front door.

ORGANIZING MY OWN SERVICES

I could no longer do any sort of work around the house and my poor mother was taking care of me. She was doing the grocery shopping, taking out the garbage, and unloading the dishwasher. Several times a day, I would ask her to pick up things on the floor that I needed like my purse or my shoes. I would also request that she get my vegetables from the crisper because I could no longer bend over. I didn't know that medical supply companies and certain pharmacies sold devices called reachers, which could pick up the objects on the floor and help me to get my socks off. Even if I had known about this useful item, the reacher would not have been able to get down into the bottom of the refrigerator to get out the broccoli. Neither could the reacher nor any other assistive device drive to the grocery store and shop for my mother and me. I found grocery shopping online to be time-consuming and expensive, so I called a number of stores in our area and asked if they would accept a weekly fax. One store agreed to do so. I would fax in the grocery order and they would deliver it to our house. What a relief that was!

However, that only solved one of my purchasing problems. I had other errands that popped up regularly that I could not do anymore. I contacted a friend, who recommended a woman that was willing to do errands for $12 an hour. I also persuaded the seniors organi-zation in my town to allow me to use their transportation service. They would take me to medical appointments, even though I was not a senior. The seniors organization was wonderful. They saved my life by driving me to physiotherapy and the doctor's office when

I was too sick to drive myself, or to use the local Paratranspo system.

Paratranspo is a transportation system designed specifically for the disabled. They pick people up at their front door and drop them off at their destination. The problem with Paratranspo is that they can take two hours to drive someone to an appointment that would otherwise take 20 minutes by car. But Paratranspo was cheap at $3.40 for a return ride whereas the seniors charged $8 to $12 per outing. My money was going out like water hiring people to do my errands. In addition, I paid a friend of the family to drive me around and my beautiful neighbor often took me to my appointments for free.

Next to my phone, I kept a master list of friends that I could call on when I needed things. I tried to rotate people so that I was not asking the same person for help repeatedly within a given week or two. During this time, I was also dating a man who was incredibly helpful to me. He offered practical assistance, moral support, and stimulating company right up until the time of my surgery.

Ironically, my date had a slight limp, which was caused by a knee injury that he incurred by playing basketball. We were in our forties and we were both limping. When I realized the dark humor in this, I said to him, "I'm not going out with you anymore. People will think that we're making fun of the disabled!" "Hey. I was limping way before I met you," he retorted. Touché.

ADDITIONAL HEALTH PROBLEMS

On top of everything else, I have a severe case of reactive hypoglycemia, or low blood sugar, which was the result of stomach surgery. Alimentary hypoglycemia is the most dangerous form of low blood sugar and can cause extreme symptoms from shaking, heart palpitations, mental confusion and drowsiness to seizures or coma. I follow a strict high protein/low carbohydrate diet, which prohibits all forms of sugar, white flour, caffeine and junk food. However, when I was upset and experiencing a great deal of pain in my hip, I would feel discouraged. Consequently, I would comfort myself with chocolate or Chinese food, which is taboo on my diet. I would pay for my transgressions all week long by having low blood sugar symptoms, which only served to aggravate my existing depression. My bad moods and constant complaints took a real toll on my family, my boyfriend, and my friends.

From September 2001 to December 2002, there were many weeks where my pain level decreased to a state that was almost tolerable, if I grossly restricted my movements and activities. I was able to do some freelance writing and to spend a six-week period working at Carleton University helping a doctoral student to analyze data for her social psychology thesis. These brief periods of respite were a relief to me but they were also confusing, and made me doubt my decision to have the joint replaced. Was it possible for me to wait just a little longer as the first surgeon had suggested? I was afraid that if I had a THR so young, I would require a second and possibly third revision surgery over the next few decades. The brief periods of remission reinforced my uncertainty about my need for the surgery, despite the enormous problems that the hip presented for me. But the remissions were to end abruptly in the beginning of 2003.

THE FINAL DECLINE

One day in January, I went to put my foot down in the kitchen but I could not extend my leg. It seemed stuck and had locked on me. My leg was suspended in the air for several minutes while I screamed with pain. I made an emergency appointment to see my surgeon. He took another set of x-rays and told me to buy a pair of crutches in order to take the weight off my hip joint. Although I had used crutches for more than seven months after my car accident, years of playing computer games had damaged my wrists, which made it impossible for me to support my body on crutches. Instead, I purchased a walker and continued to limp along on my cane.

One night shortly after seeing the surgeon, I got stuck on the stairs. I could not go up the stairs and I could not go down the stairs; I could only sit in the middle of the staircase and hold my aching hip. That night I could not get my left leg into bed. It is hard to describe but the pain was so excruciating that I could not even take the leg with my hand and move it manually into my bed. At this point, I realized that I was not going to make it through the waiting period for the surgery without some form of painkiller. I began taking OxyContin that night and stayed on it for almost six months.

OxyContin is a narcotic. It has received a lot of publicity recently because it was the prescription drug that Rush Limbaugh became addicted to. Normally, I don't even take Tylenol since I don't like taking drugs, but OxyContin was the only thing that enabled me to endure the four months before the operation. Without it, I would not have survived. Even with the medication, I began lying awake at night with pain. I could no longer extend my leg in bed and had to sleep with my left leg on top of one or two pillows.

One morning, I got up to make breakfast and dragged my chair from the kitchen table over to the refrigerator. As usual, I sat down on the chair and bent down towards the crisper to get out the bacon when I felt the most indescribable pain shooting down my back. I was paralyzed and could not move from the chair. My mother called an ambulance and I spent more than six hours in the emergency room.

The emergency room is definitely a place that the reactive hypoglycemic should avoid! Due to my low blood sugar, I have to eat every two hours and the emergency room will not permit people to eat any food at all, in case they require immediate surgery. I knew perfectly well that no one was going to operate on me for my back problem, so I felt justified in eating the small snacks that I had hidden in my purse. Unfortunately, I did not have enough food to sustain me and my blood sugar reached an all-time low.

In order to control the back pain, I was given a shot of morphine. Once again, my back had gone out because I was compensating with spinal muscles in order to avoid using my hip. My own surgeon was not available so I saw the intern who was on duty. I was distraught when he told me that there was nothing that he could do for me. I informed the intern that I could not walk at all now that my back had gone out, in addition to the deterioration of my hip joint. I begged him to admit me to the hospital for two or three days until my back recovered. He refused. I asked this doctor if he wanted me to break my hip, and told him that was exactly what was going to happen if I were sent home in this shape. He shrugged, explaining that it was not possible to move me up on the hip replacement list.

Apparently, it is common to have back and knee pain when the hip joint degenerates. In his book *All about Hip Replacement: A Patient's Guide*, Dr. Richard Trahair discusses the stories of several people who have had hip replacements, including his own. A psychologist, Trahair is interested in the mental and emotional reactions to arthritis and hip surgery, as well as physical symptoms. He states that severe arthritis of the hip can cause referred pain in several other locations. Some people that Trahair interviewed weren't even sure that their problem was in their hip because the gist of their pain was experienced in their back or knees.

THE LONG WEEKEND AT THE CONVALESCENT HOME

I spiraled into a depressive funk after the episode in the emergency room. The Rescue Squad — aka my mother, my neighbor and his wonderful wife — deposited me in a convalescent home for three days. Since I could not walk, I stayed in bed and was escorted to meals by wheelchair. The home charged $75 per day to provide me with nursing care and meals until my back spasm dissipated. It was a dismal place. An older woman sat in the foyer everyday, all day long, coughing. When I asked her what was wrong, she told me that she was recovering from pneumonia. The residents appeared to be quite ill and elderly. Some seemed to be very lonely. In fact my dinner companion asked me repeatedly if I would come back to visit her when I went home.

Once I sat in on a recreational meeting that was meant to give the residents some enjoyment. A young woman conducted the meeting. She looked as though she had just graduated from college and seemed filled with enthusiasm, despite the poor turnout. The woman asked the group to come up with words that started with different letters of the alphabet. I thought that this was condescending unless it was aimed specifically at people with Alzheimer's. I sat close to the back of the room next to a group of malcontents, who seemed to be thinking the same thing that I was. They were grumbling and asking each other, "Who does she think we are? Does she think that we're idiots?" A few people in the front of the room were actively participating and saying, "A is for apple," "A is for aardvark," and "A is for adventure." The man behind me shouted, "A is for asinine!" My sentiments exactly. His small circle of friends laughed but the young group leader appeared not to have heard him.

Just because someone is old, sick and dependent does not mean that they are stupid. I felt that if the group had been designed for people with memory loss and mental challenges, it should have been closed and should not have been billed as the morning's entertainment. On the positive side, the staff at the convalescent home was very pleasant and accommodating to me, but I was relieved to get back home and out of the wheelchair when my back recovered.

ADVOCATING ON MY OWN BEHALF

The months from January to April are a blur to me now. I began to act as my own advocate for everything that I needed, asking my surgeon for home care services and urging the home care people to send out a counselor to help me to cope better. Although I knew that reactive depression was a perfectly normal response to increased pain and restricted mobility, I was uncomfortable asking for help. If you are waiting for hip surgery, don't be embarrassed to tell your family doctor if you have been feeling depressed. Many things can be done to help you feel better emotionally while you are going through this trying time. You may wish to talk to a professional, such as a psychologist, social worker, minister or a psychiatrist, if medication is warranted. I would have gone on antidepressants but they have not helped me in the past. Instead, I opted for counseling.

Finally, I was set up with home care workers, who cooked and cleaned, as well as a visiting mental health nurse. The nurse was a proponent of cognitive behavioral therapy, something with which I am familiar since my undergraduate degree is in psychology. Cognitive behavioral therapy is based on the premise that your thoughts and actions affect your emotions. Therefore, in order to alleviate depression, one must address his or her thoughts. The nurse would suggest simplistic but sensible things for me to do. She advised me to list ten things a day that I was grateful for and to schedule something that I enjoyed into every single day, even if it was only ten minutes worth of music or a phone call to a friend. She recommended that I add more levity and enjoyment to my days and to begin concentrating on what I *could do* rather than what I *could not do*.

Thus, I began renting more comedies like "Bridget Jones's Diary," and "All about a Boy," with Hugh Grant. I watched the entire Canadian series "Newsroom" by Ken Finkleman, which was hysterically funny. I also reread classic inspirational books like Harold Kushner's "When Bad Things Happen to Good People," and newer books like "Tuesdays with Morrie," by Mitch Albom and "Heart Songs," by the late Mattie Stepanek. Cognitive behavioral therapy made me feel a little better but only the surgery itself succeeded in relieving my depressive state. The counseling simply enabled me to function better with my pain and frustration on a day-to-day basis until I was able to have the operation.

THE COST OF SUFFERING

In Canada, we have socialized medicine so I did not have to worry about the cost of the surgery. For some people, waiting lists are not an issue but finances are. McCullen and Miller state that the average hip replacement costs between $22,000 to $35,000 in the United States, making hip, knee, and ankle replacements a $6 billion a year industry. Irwin Silber, author of *A Patient's Guide to Knee and Hip Replacement: Everything You Need to Know* estimates the cost of the operation to be even higher at $35,000 to $45,000 U.S. This includes fees for the surgeon, the anesthesiologist, the hospital stay, doctor visits, and physiotherapy. Most health plans including Medicare will pay for this, but many have deductibles that must be satisfied and charge co-payments for the treatments.

Linda May-Bowser from McComb, Mississippi is the creator of an excellent web site and online support group for people with hip problems, aptly called *Totally Hip*. Along with providing a wealth of information about joint replacements and a lively discussion board, she offers T-shirts, mugs, and posters that say, "I've got a $50,000 wiggle!"

In Canada, the Institute of Health Economics estimates the cost of a hip replacement to be approximately $7000 to $10,000. However, most people are covered by the universal health care system and will not incur any hospital or doctor expenses, unless they go to a private clinic. Private clinics are available in Alberta, British Columbia, Ontario and Quebec, where the cost of a total hip replacement is about $15,000.

Australia has a two-tiered system with both public and private hospitals. Dr. Trahair only waited five weeks for his surgery after he made the final decision that he could no longer live with the pain in his hip joint. His wait was extremely short because he had private health insurance. Convalescent centers can be expensive and generally are not covered by any type of insurance, but rehabilitation units in hospitals are usually covered by the same policy that paid for the hip replacement.

DID I MAKE THE RIGHT DECISION?

On one hand, I'm glad that my hip deteriorated to such an extent, despite all of the distress that it caused my loved ones and me. If I had had my joint replaced in July of 2001 when my operation was scheduled with the first surgeon, I always would have wondered if I had acted prematurely. Thanks to the complete incapacitation that I suffered from January until April of 2003, I have no doubt whatsoever that I did the right thing by having a total hip replacement.

On the other hand, the agonizing wait for surgery took a terrible toll on me, physically and emotionally. It is a miracle that I did not fall and break my hip or any other bones during the last four months of my wait. I met several people at the swimming pool who had waited so long for hip surgery that they had fallen over, broken their hips and required surgery on an emergency basis. Everyday, I feared that I was going to be one of those people. My quadricep muscles completely atrophied, which significantly delayed my recovery post-operatively. I was angry and irritable most of the time because I could not work in any capacity, could barely walk with my cane and was in severe pain.

Many times during the 18 months that I waited for my hip replacement, I wished that I were living in New Jersey again where I would not have been at the mercy of a national health care system. Of course, I also recognized the fact that prompt and efficient medical attention is *only* available to those who are fortunate enough to be well insured in the United States.

3

Preparing for the Operation

If you are contemplating hip surgery, there are several ways to prepare yourself for a total joint replacement. The first thing that I did was to brace myself emotionally. I was not thrilled with the idea of being rendered unconscious so that a virtual stranger could slice a knife through my flesh. That thought can provoke fear in the strongest of men and women. We all deal with fear differently. Some people choose to arm themselves with information, believing that knowledge is power. Other people prefer to know as little as possible about the procedure and to rely on faith in God, medicine, fate or luck. I fell into the second category. Although I had done extensive research on ways to prevent hip surgery, I did not want to read anything about the actual operation itself until after it was over. Obtaining a graphic image of someone drilling a hole through the head of my femur, in order to knock the ball out of the socket and insert a metal object, was not my idea of a useful stress reduction technique.

Instead, I viewed the surgery the same way that I envisioned a root canal: both were necessary evils with a most beneficial outcome. I kept my mind focused on the end result and refused to think about the actual surgery itself. I was going to be free of pain! I was going to be able to walk again! Fifty years ago, that would not have been possible. I would have spent my life confined to a wheelchair, in terrible pain. I was grateful beyond words to be living in the era of joint replacements. I just didn't want to know too many details about the procedure. You may feel differently. Your questions may be answered by reading about the operation and this may assuage your fears.

Physically, I did what I could to get ready for the operation. I had given up smoking a number of years ago, which would act in my favor since smokers are more likely to suffer from complications following surgery, such as breathing difficulties. If you are a smoker, you can decrease your chances of postoperative problems, such as pneumonia by quitting cigarettes, but this must be done several months before surgery. Since you cannot smoke in the hospital, this provides an excellent opportunity to stop smoking altogether.

In terms of other bad habits, I do not drink alcohol either, which makes me pretty much of a saint, as far as I'm concerned! My main shortcoming preoperatively was that I continued to deviate from my hypoglycemia diet. Looking back, I wish that I had adhered to my prescribed regimen more strictly, no matter how difficult it was. Stabilizing my blood sugar would have helped both my physical and mental state, but I was not ready to be canonized yet. Whenever I would break my diet, I would think of the words of the great and youthful St. Augustine, "O Lord, make me chaste — but not yet."

You may benefit by doing isometric exercises to strengthen your leg before surgery. Doctors and physiotherapists often recommend this but it seemed like a Catch-22 to me. The reason that I needed the joint replaced was because it had lost its range of motion. I could not sit on a chair and raise my left leg two inches towards my chest. The muscles just would not work and the pain was too intense. I had severe muscle wasting in my left leg and my thigh looked and felt like Jello. I understood the importance of doing isometrics to strengthen my quadriceps and gluteal muscles, and to preserve my hip flexion, but this only sounded good in theory. In practice, it was impossible. The physio exercises set off a ridiculous amount of pain as did walking and swimming, so I stayed as immobile as possible during the six months preceding surgery. You may be able to remain more active and if this is the case, it will work to expedite your recovery.

It is important to avoid colds and the flu, since the surgeon will not operate if you have any kind of infection. I was downright neurotic about germs, refusing to see anyone who even sneezed in my direction. I was damned if I was going to wait a year and a half for the surgery, only to have it postponed because I had something as mundane as the common cold.

HIP-PROOFING MY HOUSE

Many otherwise benign objects may be hazardous to the post-op patient. Like a detective, I scoured the house in search of obstacles that could present a danger to me after the operation. Since I could not reach or bend down to remove most of these items myself, I enlisted helpers to rearrange throw rugs, humidifiers, books and anything else that I might trip over on the floor. My helpers moved tables so that I would have more room to ambulate when I was on a walker.

I also had as many items as possible moved up to waist level so that they would be within reaching distance for me postoperatively. After the hip replacement, I would not be able to bend forward while seated, or to reach down to the floor while I was sitting or standing; these movements would force my hip to flex more than 90 degrees, which would put me at risk for a dislocation. The way to find 90 degrees is to sit completely upright in a chair and find a position from which you are unable to do anything that you might wish to do. That's 90 degrees! It is also referred to as "Why I should wear a bib while I'm eating soup," or "Could someone please bring me the TV remote NOW before I miss the first ten minutes of *Six Feet Under*?" At 90 degrees, you cannot move forward to grab the salt shaker on the table nor can you bend down to put on your socks and shoes. You definitely cannot reach down to the floor to slip that Sinatra CD into your player, so it helps to move certain objects up higher in your den, your kitchen and your bathroom.

CLOTHES AND GADGETS

It is important to organize your wardrobe before surgery. I chose several pairs of big baggy cotton pants with drawstrings and large pockets. When you are on crutches or a walker, you will realize how valuable it is to have extra space in your pockets in order to carry things. Large aprons can be used for the same purpose; you can strap an apron around your waist and fill pockets full of essentials to be transported from room to room.

Normally, I live in sneakers or running shoes but following the surgery, I was not able to bend forward to tie my shoes for several months. I bought a pair of slip-on Aerosole sneakers, which were a godsend. All I had to do was step into them. I did not even need a shoehorn to put them on and they were sturdy enough to offer good support for walking.

Had I known about reachers, sock aids and long-handled shoehorns, I would have purchased all of these items before the surgery instead of waiting for my physiotherapist and occupational therapist to recommend them after the operation. These devices would have simplified my life and made ordinary tasks much easier.

LINING UP HELPERS

I devised a master list of friends, drivers, and paid helpers whom I could call on to help out with things like shopping, errands, transportation, and to bring necessary items to the hospital and the convalescent home. If you have a supportive spouse, relatives or other family members, you may not need a long list of helpers. My groceries were already being delivered and I cooked a few extra items and put them in the freezer. I was set up with home care, thus, I simply had to call the agency when I was ready to leave convalescence, and they would resume my services. I contacted the hospital dietitian in advance to discuss my hypoglycemia and asked her advice about how I could arrange for snacks in the hospital. And I had a long talk on the phone with the home physiotherapist, who would be coming out to see me when I arrived home from convalescence.

FINDING A CONVALESCENT HOME

Like many consumers of medicine, I have always been proactive about managing my health. I wanted to plan as much of my recovery as possible in advance. I did not want to leave the choice of a convalescent center up to the hospital social worker. My mother and friends took me to visit several convalescent homes because I had not liked the one that I stayed in during January. I knew that I would have to spend several weeks in the convalescent home after the surgery, since I live in a two-story house and I spend the better part of my time going up and down stairs. I found a very nice place that was much more cheerful than the first one that I had been in. Unlike my first convalescent center, no one in the lobby of the new home appeared to be in any immediate danger of expiring, which I took to be a good sign! I told the new convalescent home that I was waiting for a surgical date and that I would call them as soon as possible, so that they could reserve a room for me postoperatively.

BOOKING A SURGICAL DATE

By March, I still did not have a definite date for surgery. I wondered if it would ever happen. I continued to call my surgeon's office on a regular basis to find out if there had been any cancellations and to apprise him of my declining status. His assistant was always sympathetic and helpful to me, no matter how frequently I called the office. One day when I thought that I couldn't take it anymore, the assistant called to give me a date. I was to be operated on April the 23rd and was to arrive at the hospital several days beforehand for my preoperative exam. I was ecstatic and cried tears of relief.

As soon as I booked the date for surgery, the first case of severe acute respiratory syndrome (SARS) arrived in Canada. There were two or three suspected cases of SARS in Ottawa and I began to worry that my surgery was going to be cancelled. As luck would have it, my operation was actually moved up one week to April the 15th, probably because someone who was more afraid of SARS than me, cancelled their surgical date. More irony. I was becoming like Howard Hughes, germ phobic beyond belief in my zest to avoid colds and the flu, yet I was about to be admitted to the hospital, which feared an outbreak of a mysterious and potentially fatal virus.

DONATING BLOOD

Most surgical candidates are encouraged to donate their own blood before the operation. I did not do this because I am a fainter. I have passed out several times with a needle in my arm when I only had four or five tubes of blood taken. Also, I did not want to take the risk of incurring additional weakness by giving away several pints of my own blood. There is a great deal of blood loss involved in hip surgery and I was worried about becoming anemic. I decided to boost my intake of iron for an entire year in order to keep my hemoglobin levels high, and my ferritin stores in good shape. Unfortunately, this was of no help to me after the surgery, since I lost so much blood on the operating table that I needed to be transfused with two units of blood right away.

Moreover, postoperatively, my hemoglobin was in the 70s, which is very low. The normal reference ranges for hemoglobin in Canada are somewhere around 115 to 160 grams per liter, so I was quite anemic after the surgery. In the United States, the reference ranges are 11.5 to 16 grams per deciliter; women's iron requirements are slightly less than men's. Thus, it is probably wise to eat a balanced diet but boosting your iron intake will not necessarily save you from anemia. Donate your own blood, if possible.

MOVING ON TO PRE-OP

Several days before the surgery, patients are generally asked to go to the hospital for a preoperative exam. My preoperative assessment took several hours. Since I could not walk at that point, my neighbors pushed me in a wheelchair through the long corridors of the hospital. We had to go through SARS screening before we were allowed into the hospital, which was scary, but kind of a joke at the same time. The SARS screening process involved asking us to fill out a questionnaire stating that we did not have a fever or a cold and that we had not recently traveled to China. It relied entirely on the honor system and although I'm not particularly jaded or cynical, I wondered how someone would react if his or her father were upstairs dying and he or she had an ordinary cold. Would they really report this to the SARS screening team, who would then automatically prevent them from seeing their terminally ill parent? I was doubtful.

My germ phobia saved me from any type of infection and my hip pain precluded me from enjoying the life of an international traveler. Therefore, I had no problems passing the SARS screening test and I was admitted to the hospital. The meeting consisted of talking to several staff members including a nurse, an anesthesiologist, a physiotherapist and an occupational therapist. The nurse asked me a number of detailed questions about my health in general, as well as my hip. I always feel embarrassed when I have to go through the whole grocery list of my various ailments. I fear that it will take someone three days to get a handle on my complex health issues, but the nurse was efficient and understanding. She was the first person out of dozens of skilled and compassionate hospital personnel that I would encounter, and I was deeply impressed by her demeanor.

It is helpful to make a list of all of the medications that you are taking, including vitamins and herbal supplements, to bring with you to the pre-op exam. I also made a list of questions that I had about the surgery, my recovery and concerns about how the operation would affect my blood sugar and fibromyalgia. The nurse gave me a booklet especially designed for people undergoing hip surgery. It was entitled "Patient Information: Total Hip Replacement" and told me what to expect for the next five to seven days during my hospital stay. She instructed me to go downstairs to the pharmacy in the hospital after the pre-op to buy a special disinfectant soap. I was told to scrub myself well with this soap the night before the surgery, to get up early on the morning of the surgery, and bathe and scrub with the disinfectant once again.

ANESTHESIA

The anesthesiologist discussed two different options for sedation during the surgery. He told me that I could have a general anesthesia or a spinal, with a light intravenous sedation. He suggested that I have the spinal because not only was the recovery time much quicker, but also the degree of pain in the hip joint and swelling in the leg itself would be considerably less. This is particularly true for people like me with fibromyalgia. I asked him if I would be awake at any time if I chose the spinal. He said that I would be sufficiently alert so that he could tap on my shoulder and ask me how I was doing during the operation. No, thank you!

Despite the doctor's strong recommendation, I chose the general anesthetic because I could not bear the possibility of being alert during the surgery. Looking back, I wonder if this was a mistake but I could not have done it any other way. Psychologically, I was not equipped to be conscious during the procedure. Some people have an aversion to a general anesthetic. They don't like being unconscious and loathe the side effects of the more potent general anesthesia. General anesthesea may be contraindicated, in which case a spinal may work well for you.

THE PRECAUTIONS

In order for the surgeon to access the femoral head during the operation, he or she must dislocate the joint. He twists and rotates the hip, which shocks and damages the ligaments and muscles surrounding the joint. Only time will heal the injured ligaments, muscles, the joint capsule, and the soft tissues that surround the hip. The implant also requires time to secure itself to the bone. Consequently, patients must follow certain precautions following a THR. Some patients only need to abide by the precautions for six to eight weeks whereas others must continue to adhere to them for several months. It is important to comply with the precautions in order to reduce the chance of dislocating the new hip.

Generally, patients meet with a physiotherapist, who shows them how they will be getting in and out of bed after the operation, how to move from the bed to a walker, and how to go from the walker to a chair. This was easy for me to practice before the surgery since I had quite a bit more strength in my leg than I had right after the hip replacement. The physiotherapist reviewed the basic precautions that I needed to follow for the subsequent three months until my hip had healed.

There are three essential precautions to follow and I knew these so well within a few days that I was reciting them in my sleep. First, I could not twist my hip when I was standing or lying nor could I make any sudden jerking movements that might affect the joint. I was advised to move slowly in the beginning, and trust me, no one had to tell me that during the first two or three days after surgery. I was moving at the pace of a developmentally delayed snail!

Secondly, I could not cross my legs, even at the ankles, nor could I rotate my hip to the right or to the left. Both feet had to be firmly planted on the floor several inches apart when I was sitting or standing, and my operated leg was to be straight at all times, with my foot pointing up towards the ceiling when I was lying flat in bed. Additionally, I would need to sleep with a pillow in between my legs for several months to ensure that I did not accidentally cross my legs in the middle of the night. If I wanted to sleep on my nonoperated side, this was permissible if I kept the pillow between my legs.

Thirdly, as previously mentioned, I would not be able to move my hip joint beyond a 90 degree angle. Out of all of the precautions, I found this one to be the most difficult. There is ample room for movement when you are standing up so that you do not exceed 90 degrees. However, your hip is already at a 90 degree angle when you are sitting straight up in a chair or in bed. This is where the frustration and difficulty lie.

Accomplishing daily tasks, while adhering to the precautions, is the specialty of the occupational therapist or OT. During the pre-op, the OT taught me how to use a reacher to grab objects that were on the table, the bed or the floor. Eventually, I would learn how to put on my underwear and pants with the reacher. I would use a sock aid to put on my socks and if necessary, a long-handled shoehorn to put on my shoes. I received a brief demonstration with some of these items during the pre-op.

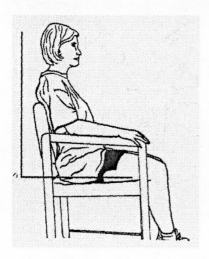

Photo of a patient sitting upright in a chair with her hip at a 90 degree angle. The caption above this picture says, "I keep my knee on the operated side at less than 70-90 degrees at all times. A cushion or pillow on the chair may assist with this." Reprinted with permission from The Ottawa Hospital, from their Orthopaedic Clinical Pathway Project Team's booklet, "Patient Information: Total Hip Replacement."

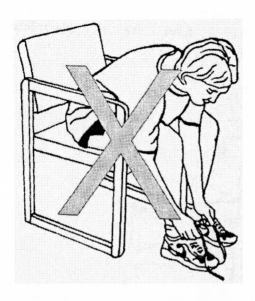

Photo of a patient bending down to tie her shoes. The caption above this picture reads, "I avoid bending forward more than 70-90 degrees." Reprinted with permission from The Ottawa Hospital.

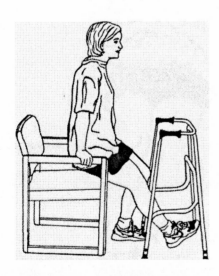

This drawing depicts the correct way to back into a chair after a THR. The pamphlet states, "I use a firm, sturdy chair with armrests. I avoid chairs with wheels, swivel chairs or rockers. I back up to the chair with my walker until I feel the back of my knees touching

it. *I move my operated leg out and keep it straight as I reach back for the armrests. I lower myself slowly into the chair. I use the same technique for sitting on a raised toilet seat." Reprinted with permission of the Ottawa Hospital.*

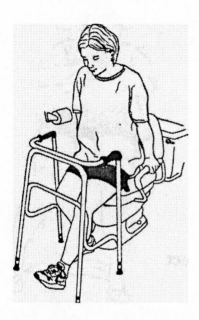

This photo illustrates the proper way to approach a toilet following surgery. Reprinted with permission of the Ottawa Hospital.

MORE TESTS

Since the THR is a major operation with a number of possible complications, people are usually screened to make sure that they do not have a weak heart, difficulty breathing, hepatitis, urinary problems, hypertension, unstable diabetes, a neurological disorder, or anything that may interfere with the success of the surgery. It is also helpful to be of sound mind in order to actively participate in the rehabilitation process. People with Alzheimer's may be poor candidates for a hip replacement because they may not be able to remember the precautions or specific physiotherapy exercises. However, the surgery is sometimes conducted on people with Alzheimer's, as is evidenced by the joint replacement given to former President Ronald Reagan at the age of 89. Besides seeing the surgeon, a consultation with the family doctor is usually conducted prior to the operation.

To ensure that my heart was in good shape, I had an EKG and passed with flying colors. My surgeon also wanted one final x-ray of my hip before the operation. I had already developed a serious aversion to the x-ray machine by the time that I reached pre-op because my pain was so acute that I could not lie flat on the x-ray table without crying. In fact, once I had to be given a shot of morphine in order for the radiologist to take the picture. Luckily, this was not necessary during the preoperative exam but I was greatly relieved to have that last picture taken. I hope that I never have to experience that kind of pain again!

4

What's Involved in a Joint Replacement?

D-Day had arrived. It was April 15th, 2003. I woke up with an overwhelming sense of dread and a strong desire to run off to Mexico. But as Fritz Perls said, "The only way out is through," so I made my way to the hospital with the help of my wonderful neighbors. Oddly, I was more worried about my low blood sugar and fibromyalgia than I was about the orthopedic end of things. I was not afraid of developing a blood clot or infection postoperatively, but I did expect to have a delayed recovery. I knew that the anesthesia, the pain medications, and the long period of fasting would destabilize my blood sugar.

Unfortunately, the anesthesiologist insisted on giving me a glucose IV since he was afraid that my blood sugar would fall too low during surgery. He was trying to act in my best interest because I would have been in trouble if I had a severe hypoglycemic episode in the middle of the operation. However, administering glucose to someone with my type of hypoglycemia was a mistake. I should have had the anesthesiologist call my endocrinologist to discuss this matter before surgery. If I had done that, I could have saved myself days of misery since the only type of IV that I should have received was a saline IV. At any rate, the inevitable hour finally arrived and I was wheeled off to the operating room.

HISTORY OF JOINT REPLACEMENTS

According to the American Academy of Orthopaedic Surgeons, Anthony White performed the first hip replacement at the Westminster Hospital in London, England in 1822. A number of different materials were used in early hip replacements including gold, ivory and glass. Artificial joints were secured with rudimentary compounds, such as plaster of Paris and glue. These replacements had a high failure rate due to infection, loosening, and the incompatibility of materials.

All kinds of replacements were tried after that, without much success. The Academy states that Philip Wiles constructed a hip replacement at the Middlesex Hospital in London in 1938. This constituted the first total hip replacement where both the femoral head and the acetabulum were replaced with metal parts. The results were not impressive. The era of the modern hip replacement did not begin until the early 1960s with Sir John Charnley at the Center for Hip Surgery at Wrightington, England. Charnley began to replace hips in the late 1950s in conjunction with Kenneth McKee, who designed the first total hip replacement to be used in North America. It took Charnley several years and many failed attempts before he perfected his surgical technique.

Charnley replaced a damaged hip socket with a plastic cup, removed the femoral head, and inserted a metal prosthesis. The socket of Charnley's hip design was made of high-density polyethylene, a hardened version of the same plastic that is used for coffee can covers. The metal extension and socket were held in place by dental cement, which is the acrylic resin polymethyl methacrylate. It was the addition of this cement that dramatically improved the way Charnley's hip replacement performed. Shortly afterwards, the artificial knee replacement was born. Dr. Frank Gunston of Winnipeg, Manitoba, who had worked with Dr. Charnley in England, was the first surgeon to perform it.

WHO NEEDS A HIP REPLACEMENT?

M.T. Simon, author of *Hip Replacements: What You Need to Know,* notes that more women undergo total hip replacements (THRs) than men, yet most hip specialists are male. This may be because orthopedic surgery is heavy work physically and the doctor needs to be strong to lift and maneuver the leg. Research in San Francisco suggests that elderly Caucasian women are the most likely candidates for hip replacement. Next are Caucasian men, black women and finally, black men. Asians are the least likely to suffer from hip disease.

A 2003 study in New Orleans confirmed the findings from San Francisco. Nizar N. Mahomed, M.D. and several cohorts examined Medicare claims to determine the relationship between certain patient characteristics and the frequency with which they had surgery. The researchers discovered that primary total hip replacements were conducted three to six times more often than revisions. The rate of both procedures increased with age, up to the age of 75 to 79 years, and then decreased. Rates were higher for women than for men, whites than for blacks, and those with higher incomes than for people with lower incomes. The incidence of complications was twice as high for patients undergoing revision surgery as it was for those who had primary hip replacements.

It is interesting to note that socioeconomic status plays a role in the frequency with which people have hip replacements. One might surmise that this is an American phenomenon, which may result when poorer patients without insurance receive inadequate medical care. However, the Toronto Rehab study by Hawker and Williams found that people with low incomes and/or less education were twice as likely to have arthritis of the hip and knee. But they were only half as likely to have their arthritic joints replaced as were more affluent individuals.

Why would such disparity occur in Canada, a country with universal health care? Hawker and Williams attributed the gap to "people communicating differently with their doctors, according to their gender and socioeconomic status." Apparently, individuals with low incomes and less formal education tend to view arthritis as a normal part of aging rather than a disease. Consequently, they may feel that arthritic pain is something that they have to live with instead of a medical condition that can be treated.

The study also revealed that women in higher socioeconomic brackets had less access to joint replacement surgery than men of similar income levels. This suggests that it is not only patients who describe pain differently according to their income level and gender. Since women tend to complain more often than men, it is possible that doctors do not take women's health problems as seriously as those of men. Consequently, physicians may perceive arthritis as being more severe and in need of treatment if the patient is a well-educated, upper class male. This finding is problematic if women are more likely to need hip replacements than men.

THE NEWLY HIP

Traditionally, total hip replacements have been done largely on older people, but in recent years younger patients and celebrities have undergone hip surgery. Linda May-Bowser, founder of the *Totally Hip Support Group*, states that celebrities who have become newly hip include actress Liza Minnelli, rock stars Eddie Van Halen and Steve Perry, Golf Pro Jack Nicklaus, Opera singer Luciano Pavarotti, and former President George Bush, Sr. and his wife Barbara. Elizabeth Taylor has already had three hip replacements; she had surgery on both hips and one had to be replaced again because her legs were of unequal length following the first operation.

Several of the aforementioned actresses, athletes, musicians and politicians were under the age of 65 at the time of their THR. According to the Canadian Institute for Health Information, patients age 50 and over account for 91 percent of all hip replacement surgeries and 97 percent of total knee replacements. At the same time, M.T. Simon asserts that people between the ages of 45 and 64 now constitute approximately 25 percent of all joint recipients.

The most common reason for a joint replacement is that the joint has been irrevocably damaged by one of several forms of arthritis. There are more than 100 different types of arthritis, which are marked by pain, stiffness, and in many cases, swelling in the joints. The National Arthritis Foundation claims that arthritis is the number one cause of physical disability, affecting nearly 43 million Americans. The Foundation notes that almost 28 million people in the United States suffer from osteoarthritis, 80 percent of whom are female. The condition is most likely to occur in people age 55 and older. 3 million Canadians are afflicted by osteoarthritis (OA), according to the Canadian Orthopaedic Foundation. By the age of 40, most of us will have OA in at least one joint and by the age of 70, almost 85 percent of Canadians suffer from this common but painful condition.

Arthritis is characterized by an inflammation of the joint, which causes a loss of bone and a degeneration of cartilage. Cartilage is a thin, tough substance, which surrounds and protects the joint. Synovial fluid acts as a lubricant for the joint, enabling it to move easily. After arthritis has set in, the articular cartilage is damaged

41

and there is not enough synovial fluid, so fibrocartilage forms along with bone spurs. As discs in the hip joint slowly wear out, ligaments loosen. The body compensates by thickening the ligaments that hold the bones together. Over time, the thick ligaments tend to calcify, which causes small pieces of bone to form. These extra pieces of bone are referred to as bone spurs or osteophytes. They signify degeneration of the joint.

When cartilage deteriorates, a person is left with bone rubbing on bone. This becomes so painful that ordinary daily activities are restricted. Many people consider osteoarthritis to be the result of the aging process whereas others, such as the Arthritis Foundation, believe that osteoarthritis is a progressive disease. It may be caused by ordinary wear and tear on the joints or by a sports injury, a car accident, or a fall. Arthritis that is caused by an injury or an accident, like my own, is often referred to as post-traumatic arthritis. Unlike rheumatoid arthritis, osteoarthritis may occur in only one joint.

Rheumatoid arthritis (RA) affects 2.1 million people in the United States and 300,000 Canadians. Women are three times more likely to get this autoimmune disease than men. Sadly, it often affects young women between the ages of 20 to 40. RA is systemic, meaning that it affects the entire body and is characterized by pain, stiffness, redness, swelling and an inflammation of the membrane lining the joint. The inflamed joint lining, the synovium, can invade and damage bone and cartilage, causing the need for the joint to be replaced.

Ankylosing spondylitis and systemic lupus erythematosus are other forms of arthritis that can destroy the joint. Additional causes of degenerative joint disease are dysplasia (a precancerous change in the cells of the hip,) gout, prolonged treatment with cortisone, osteoporosis, congenital dislocation of the hip, bone tumors and avascular necrosis. The latter is also known as osteonecrosis or loss of blood flow to the femoral head. Less common conditions that damage the hip joint include Otto's pelvis and Paget's disease. Otto's pelvis is a protrusion of the acetabulum into the pelvis, which may occur along with severe osteoarthritis of the hip. It tends to come on in puberty and often progresses to cause a severe loss of movement in the hip joint. Paget's disease of the bone is a chronic skeletal disorder, which may result in enlarged or deformed bones that are dense but fragile. All of these conditions can make an individual susceptible to a hip fracture or a deterioration of the joint that may necessitate the need for a total hip replacement.

WHAT'S INVOLVED IN THE OPERATION?

The hip joint is composed of a ball and socket. The top of the thigh bone or the femur is shaped like a ball and is referred to as the femoral head. Part of the pelvis is shaped like a cup and is called the acetabulum. The femoral head fits inside the acetabulum and is surrounded by cartilage, tendons, ligaments and nerves, which provide blood supply to the joint. During the surgery, the femoral head is removed and the acetabulum is "reamed," or drilled to create a smooth surface so that the arthritic parts can be replaced with a prosthesis. The prosthesis consists of steel components: a socket, a ball, and a stem. The outer shell of the socket is usually made of metal and the inner shell is frequently composed of polyethylene, a high-density plastic. Sometimes the entire socket is made out of plastic. The artificial ball with its stem is made of a strong stainless metal, although newer implants may use ceramic.

During the operation, the surgeon makes an eight to ten inch incision in the upper thigh. The hip is dislocated from the socket and rotated so as to expose the head of the femur, which is removed and hollowed out to make room for the prosthesis. The socket portion of the pelvis is enlarged with a drill and damaged articular cartilage is reamed out. Finally, the ball part of the prosthesis with its stem is placed on the end of the femoral component, and the stem is placed inside the femur with the ball on top. When all of the parts are in place, they are adjusted to ligaments and muscles. In order to stabilize the implant, the surgeon must decide whether or not to use cement.

The following photo is an x-ray of Linda May-Bowser's total hip revision. Originator of the *Totally Hip Support Group*, she had her left hip replaced at the age of 32, due to avascular necrosis. Dr. Audrey Tsao of Jackson, Mississippi later performed revision surgery when Linda was 47.

CEMENTED VERSUS UNCEMENTED

With the advent of the Charnley prosthesis, hip replacements were generally cemented. At that time, most replacements were performed on older people to alleviate their pain and restore mobility. Now that younger people are having THRs, there is a controversy over whether or not to continue cementing the prosthesis. A generous estimate of the average lifespan of the present-day hip replacement is somewhere between 15 to 20 years. Most doctors, including my own, give a more conservative estimate of 10 to 15 years. Thus, if a person has his or her first hip replacement at the age of 50, he or she may require one or two more revision surgeries during the course of a lifetime.

It is difficult for the surgeon to remove cement if a revision needs to be performed, therefore, many surgeons will not cement the hip of an individual under the age of 60 or 65. It may take a little longer to recover from an uncemented replacement but this type of prosthesis has the potential to permit bone to grow into it. Consequently, it may last longer than the cemented hip. Strong fixation of the implant reduces the risk of dislocation. The two main ways of fixating the implant are by using bone cement or bony ingrowth. Cemented implants use polymethyl methacrylate to secure the prosthesis whereas bony ingrowth, or uncemented implants, use a coating called hydroxyapatite to stimulate the growth of bone into the implant. A cemented hip is most useful in elderly patients, who are unlikely to require a second replacement.

5

The Hospital

My surgery took place as scheduled. I was given an uncemented hip made out of cobalt and titanium. For those who are interested in the technical details of the implant, my new hip has a titanium shell with a highly crosslinked polyethylene liner. It also has a Secur-Fit titanium stem coated with hydroxyapatite and a cobalt chrome femoral head measuring 28 millimeters.

I woke up in the recovery room, feeling as though I'd been hit by a Mack truck. I stayed there for more than five hours, which is quite unusual. Generally, people are in recovery for about two hours. However, my blood pressure fell precipitously during surgery. I'm not exactly sure why that happened but my surgeon reassured me that it was common. Moreover, thanks to the glucose IV, my blood sugar had risen to 19.2 millimoles, which is equal to approximately 350 milligrams. The normal reference range for blood sugar on the metric scale is between 4 to 6.4 millimoles per liter. In the U.S., the range is 80 to 120 milligrams per decilter. 350 milligrams is much too high! I knew that I was going to feel very ill while the law of gravity forced my blood sugar to drop back down, way below normal.

THE ORTHOPEDIC WARD

I don't remember many details about the first week in the hospital because I was extremely sick. After I was released from the recovery room, I was taken upstairs to the orthopedic ward. I had insurance to cover the cost of a private room and was disappointed to find that there was none available. Ordinarily, I enjoy talking to people and I can be quite chatty, but I feel positively antisocial when I am unwell. Luckily for me and for any prospective roommates, I had the semi-private room all to myself for two days postoperatively.

The first day of my surgery, a sweet and wonderful nurse cared for me by the name of Jean-Marc. He was an absolute angel, which seemed apropos because I felt more than half dead. I felt unbearably weak from the huge drop in blood pressure, losing so much blood during the operation and the terrible hypoglycemia from my IV. The prolonged period of fasting did not help either; people with reactive hypoglycemia have to eat frequently and of course, I had not been able to eat all day long.

PAIN

I was hooked up to all kinds of tubes including an oxygen mask, an intravenous for fluids and antibiotics, and a catheter. I had an adduction pillow between my legs in order to prevent me from crossing my legs and dislocating my new hip. And I was connected to a PCA, a patient controlled analgesic pain pump. Because I was exhausted and not thinking properly, I did not give myself enough medication. I was afraid that I would give myself too much morphine but instead I gave myself far too little. On the third day, I asked for the PCA to be terminated so that I could switch back to the oral painkiller OxyContin, otherwise known as Percocet. In my mental stupor, I mistakenly concluded that I would have more strength if I cut back on the pain medication. Wrong! Consequently, I grossly undermedicated myself and had horrific pain during the first week.

During that time, I thought a lot about the people I knew who had had hip replacements. So many people told me that the crippling pain that had plagued them before surgery disappeared afterwards. Of course, there was the pain of the incision postoperatively, but by and large, my cohorts had an immediate reduction in pain in the hip joint itself. I had also read this in several books. "There will probably be residual soreness as a consequence of the operation," cautioned Ryle Miller, veteran of both a hip and knee replacement. "Patients frequently find that the pain has gone on waking up after the operation. There is obviously discomfort from the surgery itself but this settles within a few days," advised Richard Villar.

Oh, this was too funny. As my nephews would say, "Laughing Out Loud!" Soreness? Discomfort? My leg felt as though it had been hit by a baseball bat and broken in about five different places. "Soreness" was not a word that occurred to me to describe my situation. "Agony" was more like it! Not only did my leg hurt like hell for the entire first week but it also felt like lead. I could not lift my leg on my own. All of my leg muscles had been weakened by the surgery. My leg felt as heavy as if it had been encased in a plaster cast, and I had a sharp pain in my thigh; the latter is common but not serious and disappeared over time.

OTHER UNMENTIONABLE COMPLICATIONS

To add insult to injury, the cheerful nursing staff gave me a megadose of laxatives on my second day after the operation. They assured me that I wanted to stay "regular," despite my protestations that I did not have any difficulty in that department. By the third day of my stay on the orthopedic ward, I had nonstop diarrhea, intractable nausea, and a serious case of the dry heaves. This unfortunate problem is not called "the runs" for nothing! The last thing that a weak, frail person, who cannot fully weight bear on a new hip, wants to do is to run back and forth to the bathroom. Despite unsuccessful attempts by the physiotherapist to get me out of bed on day two and three, the only thing that forced my ambulation was the laxative overdose.

However, I could not get up out of bed by myself. Every time I moved, I required assistance. I had to call a nurse to lift my aching leaden leg out of bed and help me to limp off to the bathroom with my walker. The only one who may have suffered more than me during my gastric episode was my new roommate, who had to listen to me heave and complain. Next time round, if I need a revision on my hip, I plan to take Nancy Reagan's sage advice and, "Just Say No" to laxatives.

Meanwhile, I was woken by a mild-mannered and apologetic lab technician, who appeared every morning at my bedside to draw blood to measure my Coumadin level. I was maintained on Coumadin, an anticoagulant, the whole time that I was in the hospital in order to reduce the risk of a blood clot. I was also given shots of heparin twice a day for the same purpose. Heparin kicks in faster than Coumadin to thin the blood, so the heparin was discontinued once the Coumadin started working. I loathed the heparin shots because they were given in the stomach and they really hurt. Some nurses are better than others are at giving shots. I soon learned who gave the least painful heparin shot but this information was not very useful to me, since I could not exactly request the nurse of my choice. I was thrilled when my surgeon authorized the cessation of the heparin on my fifth or sixth day post-op.

Despite the difficulty that I had keeping food down, I still received daily visits from the physiotherapist encouraging me to get up out of bed. I made a number of valiant attempts to do so but every time I stood up, I felt as though I were going to pass out. The same thing happened when I sat in a chair. I felt weak and faint and slept most of the days away. I could not practice walking up and down the corridor. Nonetheless, I did manage to perform three sets of isometric exercises in bed everyday. This included pumping my ankles up and down to keep my blood circulating, and tightening my buttocks and the quadricep muscles in my thighs. I was also strongly encouraged to do deep breathing exercises everyday to reduce the risk of developing pneumonia.

The nurses helped me with bathing after surgery. I was given a basin and was able to wash the top part of my body by myself, but because I could not bend forward, the nurses washed my legs and feet. The occupational therapist tried to teach me how to put on a huge pair of hospital pajama pants with a reacher, but in my confused and mentally exhausted state, this simple task appeared impossible. Using the reacher to put on the pants made about as much sense to me as using chopsticks to eat a bag of sunflower seeds! It seemed ridiculous and I could not envision how it could be done.

ANEMIA

My surgeon came in to see me everyday, even on weekends. He was a sharp dresser and always looked as though he were ready for a night on the town in his fine suits and ties, whereas I looked like an advertisement for a NyQuil ad. My doctor was very understanding about my slow recovery and complications. Many orthopedists cannot think beyond their own specialty, but thankfully, my man was able to take my whole situation into account. However, we disagreed about my need for a transfusion. My hemoglobin had dropped down to the 70s when I was not able to eat. It rose to about 92 grams by the end of my first week in the hospital, but that is still well below normal and I was quite anemic. (92 grams would be equivalent to 9.2 milligrams in American terms.)

I felt that my recovery was being impeded by the anemia since I could not practice my walking at all. The farthest that I could walk was to a chair in the hall that was about 30 feet away from my bed. Even the physiotherapist stopped persuading me to walk down the hall when she saw how shaky I was. She did not want me to pass out and fracture the new hip. I was already dealing with low blood sugar and fibromyalgia, which made me tired on a good day. A transfusion would have eliminated the anemia, which would have resulted in one less condition sapping my strength.

My surgeon wanted to try a more conservative route. He suggested that I take iron orally and rest for the next four to six weeks. He had already transfused me with two units of blood on the operating table, and did not want to incur a further risk of me contracting a disease from the blood bank. If I had been able to donate my own blood, I am sure that the doctor would have approved another transfusion. He was trying to protect me and I respected that. Thus, I deferred to his judgment. In retrospect, I wish that I had pushed for the transfusion regardless of the risks, or that I had forced myself to donate my own blood, despite my squeamishness. That would have saved me weeks of debility, which significantly delayed my walking.

Highlights of my first week in the hospital included extraordinarily kind and skilled care provided by the nurses and other staff members. On my sixth day post-op, I was able to take my first shower with the help of a personal care assistant. She took me down to the shower in a wheelchair and helped me to get on to a bathtub transfer bench. It felt like heaven but the amount of energy that it took to bathe knocked me out for the entire day. I received two beautiful floral arrangements: one from my mother and the second one from her thoughtful friend. Lastly, I had several erotic, drug-induced dreams about Rob Thomas, gorgeous lead singer of the rock band Matchbox Twenty. I could have had a bona fide orgy if I had only taken the recommended dose of Percocet!

On Easter Sunday, my surgeon came to see me as usual. I announced, "I couldn't feel worse if I had been nailed to the cross!" Then I smiled and added, "And I've been waiting all week to say that." We both understood that I was in no shape to go home. I asked him if he would consider referring me to the short-term rehabilitation unit in the hospital and he agreed right away. Most people who have hip replacements do not stay in the hospital for the length of time that I did. After six to ten days, they are ready to meet with a social worker to make discharge-planning arrangements for home care, physiotherapy, and occupational therapy to visit them at their house.

WEEK TWO

My second week in the hospital was much less eventful than the first week. All of the tubes were gone — catheter, oxygen mask, IV pole — except for my heplock, a small needle that remained in my hand, so that the lab technician could draw blood every morning to monitor my need for Coumadin. My biggest problem during the second week continued to be extreme weakness. Every time I stood up to walk in the hallway, I felt as though I were going to faint. Every afternoon, I fell asleep. I could hardly talk on the phone and did not want to see anyone, which was a good thing because due to the SARS scare, no one was allowed to have any visitors during their first two weeks in the hospital.

ROOMMATES

I had a series of roommates and two of them had total hip replacements. My first hip roommate had a revision. Her primary hip replacement had become infected so she needed to have it removed. The woman, who was in her seventies, slept for several days after her surgery until she received a transfusion. The very next afternoon, she was wide-awake. The difference in her was like night and day, and she was able to do much more walking than I was. She was more stable on her feet and had infinitely more energy. No wonder David Bowie and the Rolling Stones used to have transfusions to rejuvenate themselves! It was hard to tell who the senior citizen was in my room. I was lying lifelessly in bed while a woman 28 years older than me was cruising up and down the hospital corridors.

My new roommate also had considerably less pain than I did, probably because she was taking eight Percocets a day. I was down to one Percocet per diem and was trying to wean myself off the medication completely. That was a terrible mistake. All I could think of were the books that I had read and the people I had talked to, who said that their pain diminished immediately after surgery. They had been able to discontinue their medications in a short period of time.

Throughout my entire hospital stay and well into my recovery process, I made the error of comparing myself to other people and to this "gold standard" of recovery from a THR. It took months for me to realize that many people fall outside of the perimeters of the gold standard and recover on their own timetables. One day, I was in so much pain that all I could do was lie on my side and cry. A kind and knowledgeable nurse took the time to talk to me and dispel me of the notion that the pain "should" have been gone by then. She encouraged me to go back on a modest dose of Percocet, which made a significant difference in my pain level. The extra medication did give me side effects, including drowsiness, but that was simply the price that I had to pay for greater comfort.

COUNSELING

I was still feeling depressed after the surgery, so I contacted the Chaplain's Office and asked if I could speak to someone. A minister started coming to see me regularly. She was an earnest, understanding and intelligent woman, who gave me a tremendous amount of encouragement during my hospital stay, even though I am not really a believer. I am more of a "wanna-be believer," or as Woody Allen would say, "a hopeful agnostic." Nonetheless, it helped to talk to the chaplain since she was a good listener and enabled me to put my problems back into perspective.

All of my anger for the drunk driver who hit me returned. I realized that forgiveness was a process much like grief. Although I had forgiven him years before, the deterioration of my hip joint and the strain of going through the replacement, brought all of my negative feelings towards him back to the surface again. Mothers Against Drunk Drivers provides an excellent pamphlet entitled, "Don't Call Me Lucky" by Dorothy Mercer, Ph.D. and Janice Harris Lord, ACSW. It discusses the many grief cycles of a person whom a drunk driver has injured. "You start a new grief cycle every time you learn more about the seriousness of your injury. Grief cycles begin again each time you try to do something you thought you could do, and fail."

51

In my case, grief began anew when my hip collapsed on me in November of 2000, almost 20 years after my car accident. Both the chaplain and the mental health nurse helped me to work through these feelings so that I could move forward emotionally.

Most of the second week in the hospital involved waiting and resting. I was to be transferred to the rehabilitation unit and was waiting for an available bed. Finally, I managed to get the huge pajama bottoms on with a reacher and to sit up in a chair every night after dinner to watch *Friends*. I never knew that watching a sitcom could be such hard work! Sitting up was exhausting and painful. Although I was grateful to be going to rehab, I dreaded it because I felt too weak to do any aggressive form of exercise.

6

Rehab and Convalescence

I had ambivalent feelings about going to the rehab unit. On one hand, I was very excited and eager to begin the intensive physiotherapy. On the other hand, I was still so exhausted and drowsy that all I wanted to do was sleep the day away. The rehab staff consisted of a family doctor, a physiotherapist, an occupational therapist, a social worker and a physiatrist, or doctor of physical rehabilitation medicine.

PHYSIOTHERAPY

Much to my surprise, I hated physiotherapy. I hadn't had any difficulty with physio following my car accident but after the hip surgery, the new exercises really hurt. I was still doing the ankle pumps, the gluteal squeezes, and the isometrics for my quadriceps. I was also lying flat on my back and extending my operated leg out to the side in order to work my abductor muscles. And I had to practice bending my knee because my knee had become painful to move since the surgery. I was taking two to three Percocets a day, as my pain level had greatly increased during my third week in the hospital when my leg started to swell like a balloon.

My knee was swollen and resembled a cantaloupe and my foot hurt so much that it felt as though someone had smashed it with a hammer. The physiatrist suggested that I start wearing the anti-embolism stockings, known as TEDs. I couldn't put the stockings on myself because I couldn't bend forward without violating the 90 degree precaution. A nurse had to put the stockings on for me in the morning and take them off at night. The TEDs worked quickly to decrease my swelling, although they didn't resolve the problem entirely. Nonetheless, it would have made a big difference to me if I had been given the stockings right after surgery.

The persistent pain and swelling made both walking and exercising difficult so I was not a happy camper in my dealings with the new physiotherapist. She was a kind and gentle but firm professional, who strongly encouraged me to walk to the gym by myself each morning. The gym was only 250 feet from my room but I gave the physio a hard time about walking that distance, since I kept feeling like passing out. Fortunately, she was gracious about my irritability and lack of enthusiasm.

The new physio provided me with a walker with wheels and a seat. Many people my age use crutches but some, like me, find it difficult to support their body weight on them. The walker offered two distinct advantages over crutches. First, I could sit down on it whenever I felt weak. Knowing that I could do this enabled me to walk much farther than I would have gone if I had not had the seat. Secondly, I could carry all kinds of things on the walker because the seat acted like a tray. It was important to find a way to carry my food, books, newspaper, and other objects when I was dependent on the walker. A hot cup of tea could easily be placed on the seat of the walker and transported from the dining room back to my hospital room, whereas I could not have carried a hot beverage if I had been on crutches.

The walk from my room to the dining room was about 70 feet but to me it felt like walking from Ottawa to Toronto. The hospital kitchen supplied me with extra food for my frequent feedings but I needed to supplement this with two additional snacks per day. When I was in orthopedics, I would simply push my call button and ask the nurse to bring me my 3:30 p.m. snack. When I tried the same tactic in rehab, I was met with an unexpected response from the nurse I affectionately deemed "Nurse Ratched." Nurse Ratched explained to me that I would be making my own afternoon snack from now on. She ushered me down to the dining room to show me how to boil water for my herb tea.

My blood sugar was very low at that point. Walking the 70 feet was so difficult that I ended up slurring my words and crying for about ten minutes until I was able to get some food into my system. Of course, I knew that the rehab nurse was only pushing me for my own good, but in the beginning, it was a painful and frustrating experience.

My new occupational therapist was warm, upbeat and extremely supportive. By now, I was able to dress myself by putting on my pants with a reacher and by using the sock aid for my socks. I had already been instructed on the importance of using a raised toilet seat by the nurses in orthopedics; I was also advised to sit on chairs that had been elevated by pillows and to avoid low surfaces. Doing so would enable my hip to remain at a 90 degree angle. The occupational therapist reinforced the importance of the precautions. She showed me how to make meals in a simulated kitchen and how to use a bathtub transfer bench. Also, the OT listened to me whine and was helpful and sympathetic.

AMUSING MYSELF

At this point, I was finally able to have some visitors and I was ready for them. I saw my mother and a number of my good friends. It was so nice to see people from my old life again. One brought me a beautiful plant with yellow flowers that lasted almost a month. My sister wired special flowers from Los Angeles and collected 20 to 30 e-mails from her friends and colleagues wishing me well. That really cheered me up! My brother and his wife called regularly from Florida to offer encouragement and to receive updates on my health.

I was also able to watch more television, which had been too difficult for me during the previous weeks. Normally, I need my daily dose of CNN. I have to know what is going on in the world even if the news is dismal. But I found myself completely unable to concentrate on the news in the hospital. In fact, I had no interest in it whatsoever except for the occasional bulletin on the Laci Peterson case.

My favorite TV shows are dramas. I enjoy a strange assortment of programs, such as *The Sopranos, Crossing Jordan, Oz, Nip Tuck,* and *Queer as Folk.* The problem with most of these shows is that they start at 10:00 p.m. and I was exhausted during my hospitalization, yearning for sleep at 9:00 o'clock. I began to watch lightweight programs like *Everybody Loves Raymond* and *Friends.* I confess that on a number of occasions, I even watched *Blind Date,* something that I would have turned off immediately if I had been feeling normal. But these comedies were great since they were cute, funny and so vacuous that they required little concentration. I didn't need Norman Cousins to remind me that laughter is good for the soul, lifts one's spirits, improves immune function, is a good distraction from pain, and simply made me feel better.

Other things that I did to pass the time included crossword puzzles and listening to books on cassette. I called the hospital library and they brought me a wide selection of books and music on cassette, along with a tape recorder. Listening to these recorded books enabled me to lie down and relax. The hospital library had some decent fiction as well as several light, trashy romance novels in paperback, which helped to kill the time. No Robin Cook or David Shobin for me at that point, although I am currently reading a good medical mystery by Shobin since I am finally past the point of being disturbed by lurid hospital stories.

I spent a lot of time talking to my new roommate. She was a woman in her seventies, who had been in good health until a man knocked into her in a shopping mall. The impact caused her to fall and break her hip. Her hip was replaced and she was sent to the short-term rehab unit because her husband had heart problems, and was unable to care for her at home. Both my roommate and I disliked calling the nurses for assistance because we wanted to do things ourselves.

One day, I noticed that my roommate's walker was sitting in front of her bed, far from her reach. With horror, I watched her bend all the way forward, grab her walker and slide it towards the side of her bed. "Look," she exclaimed triumphantly. "I didn't have to call the nurse." "No," I replied wryly, "but I might have had to call the coroner." Obviously, my roommate would not have died by bending forward like that but she certainly could have dislocated her new hip.

It worried me to think that my roommate and I could follow the precautions to the letter of the law 98 percent of the time, but if we inadvertently violated them, we risked catastrophic consequences. I was relieved when my occupational therapist told me that the new hip was not likely to dislocate if patients surpassed 90 degrees a few times. Dislocations tended to occur more often when patients had flagrantly disregarded the precautions and had made several movements simultaneously, such as flexing the hip beyond 90 degrees with adduction (crossing one leg over the other while sitting or standing) and rotation. Nonetheless, for several months I was preoccupied with the need to maintain my hip at a 90 degree angle in order to protect the new prosthesis.

WEEK FOUR – THE IMPORTANCE OF PACING

No doubt about it — I'm a Type A Personality. I used to say this with pride but now I realize that being a driven person or a perfectionist can be a great hindrance to recovery. Whether an illness or injury is chronic or acute, it is critical to learn the art of pacing yourself. If the physiotherapist recommends that you do three sets of exercises a day with 10 repetitions of each exercise, there is no reason to believe that you will feel better if you do 20 repetitions. In fact, chances are good that if you overdo it with exercise or any other activity, you may increase your pain, injure yourself, and possibly delay your healing.

I had to learn how to recognize my limits during this postoperative period. There were many things that I could do perfectly well. There were other things that I could not do at all. And there were a large number of things that fell inside a shade of gray, where I was not sure whether I could do them or not. Some things could be done once but not twice. For example, at the beginning of week four, I was finally able to walk back and forth to the gym without the physiotherapist's assistance every morning. That meant that I was walking about 500 or 600 feet return trip. I could do that walk once a day but I could not repeat it in the evening, although I tried. I had to be content with having mastered the walk in the first place rather than frustrating myself with my inability to do that distance twice a day.

On the other hand, it was just as important for me to set realistic and attainable goals as it was to force myself to rest or relax. Recovery from a total hip replacement requires a significant amount of effort on the part of the patient. Immediately after my operation, I began to set daily goals, which had to be readjusted if I failed to achieve them. Eventually, I learned to set small but achievable goals so as to avoid discouragement, and as soon as I had mastered them, I was on to the next set. Often I would stop to reflect on how much progress I had made from one week to the next.

A lesson that I learned the hard way is that after the surgery, I needed to think out every task before setting out to do it. Let's say that I was going to have a shower. I didn't just walk off to the bathroom. First, I had to make sure that I had everything with me that I would need. Did I bring my socks or slippers? Had I remembered the reacher? Although, I am rarely in the habit of dropping soap in the shower, after I had the hip replaced, I seemed to drop my soap on a regular basis. Go figure! This probably had something to do with the fact that postoperatively, I only had one hand for bathing because the other hand was holding the hand-held shower. Unless I wanted to call someone to pick up my soap, it was helpful to have my reacher with me in the bathroom. I could also have purchased a large bar of soap on a string, especially designed for the post-op patient who drops the soap, and cannot bend to the floor to pick it up.

Things began to get a bit easier for me during my fourth week in the hospital. It was about time! I was able to get back and forth to the dining room for all of my meals and to walk to the gym without difficulty in the morning. I developed a sincere affection for most of the staff members and was particularly pleased with my occupational and physiotherapist. Although I had been a difficult patient, the steady encouragement from my physio paid off and I benefited greatly by her knowledge and persistence. She taught me how to "make every step a good step." I'm still conscious of this today when I'm walking in the mall or outside. I try to stand tall and walk evenly with my weight distributed on both legs. Nurse Ratched disappeared. I realized that the tough attitudes of some of the rehab nurses were simply designed to make me do the work that would ultimately put me back on my feet.

Lastly, I learned gratitude in the rehab unit by comparing myself to the other patients in the dining room. Two people there had limbs amputated. One of them didn't speak English. Another had lost most of her vision due to macular degeneration and had just undergone a total knee replacement. I thought that these people were very brave. Every night I breathed a sigh of relief that I still had a leg to complain about.

By now, my hemoglobin had risen to 112 grams — or 11.2 milligrams in American terms — and the hospital was ready to discharge me, but I didn't feel capable of going home. I live in a two-story house and I still didn't feel steady on the stairs. I called the convalescent home that I had chosen before the surgery, but they were booked because my operation had taken place a week earlier than expected. By skimming through the Yellow Pages, I found another excellent residence and made arrangements to go there for a few weeks. I could have relied on the rehabilitation unit's social worker to make these plans for me, but I was more comfortable making them myself.

The hospital discharge planner took care of all of the necessary details of my departure like making sure that I had the correct walker, a raised toilet seat, a bathtub transfer bench, and a hand-held shower device. She was affiliated with Community Care Access Centres (CCACs,) which are funded by the Ministry of Health and Long-Term Care; one of the functions of the CCAC is to assess and arrange for visiting health and professional services in people's homes. The discharge planner made provisions for a health care worker to come to see me every morning in the convalescent center to help me to get dressed, bathe, and get down to breakfast.

CONVALESCENCE

On May the 22nd, 2003, I left the hospital and was admitted to a private retirement home that offered convalescent services. Leaving the hospital and getting into a car was quite an ordeal. It involved me backing into the car seat as though I were going to sit down in a regular chair. Instead of holding on to the arms of a chair, I held on to the doorjamb of the car as I carefully lowered myself on to the seat. Before I sat down in the car, my occupational therapist lowered the front seat on the passenger side, so that the back of the seat was leaning all the way down. My job was to slide into the car without lifting and bending my leg, and to keep my knee lower than my hip. This meant that I almost had to sit on the gearshift and lie down in order to get my long legs into the passenger seat. Deja vu! It felt like Trendelenberg.

I thought that it would have been easier for me to get into the back seat of the car and put my legs up on the seat. But this is an unsafe position because I could not strap myself into a seat belt. Once I managed to get inside the car, I propped myself up with pillows and extended my operated leg straight out. If I had bent the leg and assumed a normal sitting position, my knees would have been higher than my hips and I would have been violating the infernal precautions.

My OT gave me a little kiss on the cheek when we said goodbye, which made me happy. I was relieved to think that I hadn't been such a terrible patient after all, despite my multiple complaints and the relatively slow recovery for my age.

The convalescent home was aesthetically attractive with beautiful paintings and a large dining room with a pleasant atmosphere. For lunch, I was served fresh trout with a large salad. What a change from the hospital cuisine! I was nervous about being there for the first couple of days because everything seemed so inaccessible. Whereas the dining room in the hospital rehab unit had been about 70 feet away from my room, the dining room in the retirement home was 500 feet away. Also, I had requested a refrigerator in my room so that I could prepare my own snacks, but the fridge was positioned in such a way that I could not bend down to get my food without surpassing 90 degrees.

Moreover, I could not open the door to my room by myself because the door would not stay open; it closed on its own unless someone held on to it. Maintenance to the rescue! Within hours, the maintenance crew moved the refrigerator so that I could get into it, and changed the spring on the door so that it would stay open. That relieved a lot of my anxiety.

The Community Care Access Centre had all of my essential equipment waiting for me including my walker, the bathtub transfer bench, a hand-held showerhead, and a raised toilet seat. The maintenance crew at the convalescent home also installed the last two devices.

My room was large and spacious and was equipped with several comfortable chairs with arms. At night, I would put a pillow on the chair, kick back and rest my aching bones. Now I had a TV with 71 cable channels and I was able to stay awake until 10: 30 p.m. For the first time in weeks, I got to watch some episodes of *Oz* and *Queer as Folk*. It was enervating to get my weekly dose of Gale

Harold and Dean Winters, but I always fell asleep before the shows finished, so I never knew what happened in the end.

My exhaustion persisted and I continued to sleep away most of the afternoons. In the morning, I would wake up at 7:00 a.m. and wait for the nurse's aide to help me bathe and dress. She would take me down to the dining room by wheelchair. I only used the wheelchair for breakfast. I used my walker to get to all of my other meals and appointments, but I still felt weak in the morning due to my low blood sugar. Also, my hemoglobin is normally about 130 grams or 13 milligrams, and it had only risen to 112 grams or 11.2 milligrams by the time that I was discharged from the hospital. Technically, I was no longer anemic but my iron levels were significantly lower than the levels that my body was accustomed to having.

My companions in the dining room were almost deaf and our conversations resembled a Monty Python skit:

ME: Delicious trout today.
1ST RESIDENT: No, I haven't been out today.
ME: No, I was talking about the food.
1ST RESIDENT: What about my suit?
2nd RESIDENT: Were you talking to me?

And so on. I felt so badly for them! There is nothing funny about hearing loss. What a terrible frustration it would be not to be able to hear people talking. How many of our bodily functions we do take for granted.

I spent a lot of time sitting in the Great Room socializing with the residents during the day. I played bingo and dominos with the retirees. Needless to say, these are not my favorite activities, but distraction is a wonderful pain management tool and I needed to pass the time. I found the residents to be delightful. Old people are just young people trapped in older bodies! I formed a special friendship with a sweet 85 year-old man, who had volunteered to escort me to meals. He was a great help.

Altogether, I spent three weeks at the retirement home and my walking improved dramatically there. I had an excellent physiotherapist, who saw me once a week, and I put myself on my own walking program. I asked the nurses how many feet were in one corridor. They found a floor plan, which stated that there were 200 feet in each corridor. Every morning after breakfast, I walked 600 to 800 feet. I also tried to get my daily dose of fresh air unless it was raining outside. Until I was deprived of sunshine and fresh air, I had no idea how amazing it felt to sit — even on my walker — and soak up a few rays of sunshine.

At night, I put ice on my swollen knee and foot. Sometimes, I would elevate my operated leg to further reduce the swelling. I found it hard to believe that my entire leg was still swollen and painful two months after the surgery. Nonetheless, I took myself off the Percocet completely during the day, but continued to take my evening dose. This increased my pain at first but after five or six days, it began to calm down. I was relieved to finally be off that daytime painkiller.

Friends came in droves and I was happy to see them. Since I can't eat sweets, they treated me to special protein dishes. One friend brought an entire barbecued chicken and another hand delivered a freshly grilled steak. They arrived with books and puzzles. My thoughtful mother brought me necessities and called every morning. I was blessed to have a wealth of emotional support and practical assistance. After three weeks of good food, lots of walking moderated by ample rest, and a relatively normal hemoglobin level, I was ready to go home.

WHAT I WOULD HAVE DONE DIFFERENTLY

Although I am silently praying that I will not need revision surgery, if I had to do the whole THR over again, I would do certain things differently. First, I would not have waited so long for the surgery. Waiting until I was incapacitated caused me much needless suffering and destroyed my muscular strength. If and when my current implant fails, I will sign up for surgery right away and I will be more cognizant of the fact that waiting times for joint replacement are prohibitive in Ontario right now.

Secondly, I would never have a glucose IV. I would make sure that my endocrinologist conferred with my surgeon and my anesthesiologist preoperatively to ensure that my blood sugar remained stable. Thirdly, I would request the anti-embolism stockings immediately after surgery so as to reduce the amount of swelling and bruising in my leg.

Since I did not do well on the patient controlled pain pump, I would ask for injections of morphine and I would take all of the oral painkillers as prescribed. I really undermedicated myself, which resulted in much unnecessary distress. And I would certainly pass on the laxatives!

I also wish that I had opted for the spinal anesthesia because I suspect that I would have had less pain and drowsiness postoperatively. However, spinals are not always an option during revision surgery, since revisions are more complex to perform than primary hip replacements and take much longer. It is better to take advantage of the regional anesthesia the first time around.

Lastly, I would try to donate my own blood. If I felt too weak to donate, I would encourage my surgeon to let me have a transfusion after the operation, if I were anemic. There are risks involved in receiving blood from the blood bank but they are minimal. I would be willing to take these risks since I believe that the anemia slowed my recovery more than any other single factor, including my fibromyalgia and hypoglycemia.

If you are considering hip surgery, some of my suggestions may not apply to you. You probably do not have fibromyalgia or low blood sugar. You may do very well on the patient controlled pain pump. Many people do. You might have a high tolerance for oral medications, in which case Percocet or Vicodin may not give you adverse side effects. It is likely that your surgeon will place you in anti-embolism stockings right away and if you have donated your own blood, the doctor is not apt to withhold a transfusion. However, you may have other health issues, such as diabetes, heart problems, high blood pressure, or other arthritic joints. Simply being aware that hip surgery can result in pain, swelling, and weakness from blood loss will help you after the operation because you will want to do everything in your power to prevent and control these problems.

7

There's No Place Like Home

I was excited to be home and away from institutional settings. However, the transition from the retirement home to my own house was predictably difficult. First, I arrived before the essential equipment, which meant that I spent hours without the raised toilet seat. Since the toilet seats in my house are extremely low, it was risky to use them without violating the 90 degree precautions, but nature called and I was forced to do so. Luckily, my physio at the convalescent home had informed me how to use a low seat in the event of an emergency; I had to back into the seat and lower my body down while extending the operated leg straight out. If I did not bend my leg while seated on the low surface, I would not have to raise my knees higher than my hips. This would enable me to adhere to the precautions.

I had feared that I would have trouble navigating the stairs, but they proved to be simple as long as I went up and down one stair at a time, rather than taking one stair after another. My big problem was that all of the surfaces in my house were too low to sit on. In the hospital and the convalescent home, the chairs were higher. I could raise them even further by putting a pillow on a chair or by sitting on a large piece of foam. At home, one pillow was not enough to elevate my couch and two pillows made me feel like Alice in Wonderland after she swallowed the potion that made her too tall. My pain level increased considerably after I got home until I called a furniture store and ordered two four-inch, high-density foam cushions. I used those for about a month before I was able to return to using one pillow on top of the chair or sofa. I also experimented with taking one of the cushions from the end of my couch and putting it on top of the portion of the sofa that I was sitting on.

Standing for long periods to cook was difficult so I relied on my personal support worker, Sarah, to cook and clean for me. I also continued to think out every task before I performed it. In the kitchen if I were preparing a snack, I would review all of the necessary steps involved before I walked over to the table. Did I have my water? Had I brought the silverware? Was the salt shaker on the table? It seemed silly and mundane to spend time thinking about such trivia, but anything that saved me several trips back and forth on my walker was worth the time and effort.

In her book *Getting Back on Your Feet: How to Recover Mobility and Fitness after Injury or Surgery to Your Foot, Leg, Hip or Knee*, Sally Pryor recommends a number of helpful tips for people with mobility problems. I relied on many of Pryor's suggestions, including wearing an apron on the stairs so that I could transport bags of peanuts or bottles of water in the large pockets of the apron. I also used plastic bags from the grocery store. I could carry books, newspapers and assorted contraband easily in a large plastic bag whether I was on a walker or a cane.

With the help of yet another wonderful physiotherapist, I was soon walking almost one-quarter of a mile a day on my walker. That didn't seem like much compared to other people who were able to walk a mile or two, or who had already thrown away their canes and crutches by this time. On one hand, I felt inadequate when I compared myself to those whose recovery was so much faster than mine. On the other hand, I was jubilant that I was able to walk at all and after months of confinement, I loved being outdoors. I knew how much work I had put into my recovery and I realized that my situation was different from that of other people. I had multiple health challenges and my muscles had atrophied over the years due to forced inactivity. Moreover, my walking was extremely limited after the surgery due to the anemia. Eventually, I came to accept the fact that we all recover on our own timetables. It was only by doing so that I was able to celebrate my accomplishments and to be proud of the fact that I could now walk one-quarter of a mile. I was finally getting to know my neighbors. Before the surgery, I had discouraged conversations with the neighbors because I couldn't stand up to talk. Now, I was making up for lost time.

The physio gave me permission to take some time off from exercising when the pain became extreme. Her advice was invaluable because my tendency was to continue to push myself, regardless of the amount of discomfort involved. Since I was still having a lot of pain on a daily basis, the home physio suggested that I take a short break before I went off to outpatient physio at the hospital. This helped my pain level considerably.

MAY I HAVE YOUR VISA NUMBER, PLEASE?

Even though I live in the land of socialized medicine, the hip replacement was expensive for me. It cost over $1,000 to stay in the convalescent center. In addition, I had to rent or buy all kinds of equipment, starting with a special hand-held shower nozzle, two raised toilet seats, a bathtub transfer bench, three walkers (!), a cane, two reachers and a sock aid. Some of these items were subsidized by Community Care Access Centre but I paid for most of them. Why did I need three walkers? Well, I needed one for the main floor of my house. Then I needed a second one for the upstairs since walkers cannot be used on the stairs. I could not transport my walker outside either and down the three steps into the garage because the four-wheeled walker was too heavy to carry. Thus, I rented a third walker for my walks outdoors, which I left in the garage. It seemed absurd to have so many walkers but it was the only scheme that I could devise that allowed me to walk outdoors. An alternative plan would have been to sleep downstairs but I wasn't keen on that idea. Luckily, I had my surgery in April. It was late May or early June before I was able to start walking outside and that was truly the most beautiful time of year to exercise in Ottawa.

USEFUL TIP

It will not help to swear at your sock aid! Much like your computer, your sock aid cannot hear you and does not care that you had to spend 12 minutes getting on your left sock. It is worth the money to invest in a high quality sock aid. I had to buy two because the first one that I bought was hopeless and kept getting stuck to the back of my leg. My second one was a little better, but there were still some days when I didn't feel like changing my socks at all because of the difficulty involved.

HIGHLIGHTS OF THE 1ST MONTH AT HOME

My surgeon finally gave me permission to drive about ten weeks after the operation, which meant that I could get to my beloved library, the video store and the park. I was just weaning myself off the walker and on to a cane around this time. Once I was stable on the cane, I was able to go out for lunch, coffee and to restaurants. But I was careful to limit my fluids since most of the restaurants had impossibly low toilet seats, even in the handicapped stalls. I felt like a backpacker because everywhere I went I had to bring several items including the high-density foam cushion, my water bottle, a snack for my blood sugar, and my cane. It may sound strange to refer to the cane as something that I had to "bring with me." But the cane took up the use of my right hand and the pillow took up my left hand, so I wasn't able to carry anything else with me when I went out, including a purse. I started wearing one of those small packs that strap around the waist, which was very convenient. Finally, my leg movements became more automatic and hours would go by when I was not thinking about my hip.

My younger nephew had started a web site, which was basically a teenager's diary or rant. Of course, I'm biased, but he is a brilliant kid with a terrific sense of humor and an innate gift for writing. After reading his home page, I decided that I wanted to start my own web site about my total hip replacement. My nephew, who was 14 at the time, showed me how to create a web site like his and Sigrid's Recovery was born (http://sigridsrecovery.blogspot.com.) I began receiving all kinds of e-mails from people who had had total hip replacements. Most people had a much easier time than I did but some had complications that made their surgery more difficult than mine. Several had multiple joint replacements and many wrote to ask me how I made the difficult decision to have the operation. How had I known when I was ready? What other forms of treatment had I tried before I resorted to a THR? It was interesting to chat with other total hippers and to compare stories.

NATURE'S OWN PROZAC

By the time that I had settled into the convalescent home, my depression had lifted. Even at the height of my greatest distress immediately following the surgery, my spirits were buoyed by the constant presence of other people. When my hip deteriorated and I lost my mobility, I became isolated, which was a contributing factor to my black mood. The visiting mental health nurse came to see me at the convalescent home. I told her that I felt much better and would not need her services anymore. Being cautious, the nurse suggested that we have one more follow-up appointment once I got home, just to make sure that I felt strong again emotionally. She came out to see me at the house in June of 2003 and was pleased with both my physical and psychological progress. At that point, she discharged me from the mental health counseling program.

"SNAP BACK TO REALITY. OH, THERE GOES GRAVITY."
Eminem

Just as things were beginning to improve for me, reality intruded and I was forced to spend an inordinate amount of time attending to a series of broken appliances and arguing with service people. Appliances have an uncanny ability to communicate with one another. Although they are a mystery to those who service them, ordinary household appliances can send secret signals to each other indicating that it would be quite a lark for the total hip patient if they should all break down at the same time.

My techno problem started when I attempted to build in some relaxation time to my day by lying down and listening to a talking book. My tape recorder ate one of my tapes and it became apparent that I would need to replace the machine. With reluctance, I grabbed my cushion and my cane and limped off to the local appliance store where I had purchased my portable headset phone. The headset phone had given me a near nervous breakdown because it gave off a loud buzzing noise, which could be heard by everyone I called but naturally, the noise never occurred when I brought the phone into the store. I returned the headset phone at least five times since the store only exchanged merchandise and did not offer cash refunds. The manager and I were both delighted when inexplicably, the fifth phone worked and we no longer had to bicker over this issue.

Fortunately, the manager was not on duty when I crept into the store one Sunday afternoon and located a voice-activated tape recorder. Remarkably, it worked. I was able to lie down in peace and listen to the end of *A Widow for One Year* by John Irving.

Shortly after purchasing the recorder, I decided to buy a pedometer. Since I had graduated from the walker to the cane, I was eager to know exactly how far I was walking. Off I went to the athletic shop. I was excited to be literally counting every step that I took with my cane. One day, the pedometer said that I had walked a mile! I was thrilled. That seemed like excellent progress compared to the quarter of a mile that I had been doing on my walker. The next day I took the same walk and the pedometer registered 1649 steps, which it claimed was the equivalent of .03 of a mile. Was this the New Math? I got out my calculator and soon realized that 1649 steps were much closer to .5 of a mile. Time to return the pedometer.

Could I coordinate this trip with the broken VCR? My VCR was under warranty but because of the hip surgery, I could not lift or carry it downstairs. I called the boy next door and he kindly put the VCR in my car. I was pleased that I managed to get the machine into the appliance shop by myself only to be told that they no longer serviced VCRs. They had contracted out to a local repair shop, which was out of my driving range. I hired a woman to take the VCR down to the new store, which looked to be the size of my kitchen.

Meanwhile, my scanner stopped working. Cleverly, I decided that I would fix this matter myself in order to avoid the grief of dealing with yet another service person, and the expense of hiring someone to do things that I would normally do myself. Reloading the scanner software did not work so I reformatted my hard drive. In order to save my data, I copied half of it to floppies and sent about 40 e-mails from my regular e-mail account to my Yahoo! account so that they would be stored for me on the Web. Not only did the reformatting fail to resolve the problem, but when I went to check my Yahoo! account, I only had four new e-mails instead of 40. Who knows who received the other 36 e-mails? Hope that I didn't send those naked pictures of myself off to Aunt Marg!

While other people were experiencing distress during the major power outage that paralyzed the East Coast in August of 2003, I was feeling greatly relieved. For once, I knew why my appliances weren't working. Both my hip and I took a much needed break during the brief power shortage.

SAY GOODBYE TO 90 DEGREES

Three months after my THR, the precautions were finally discontinued. But I had become so accustomed to keeping my hip at a 90 degree angle that I found it hard to make myself move forward or to bend down. Like the characters in the movie *The Awakenings*, who would suddenly slide into a catatonic state, I would freeze at 90 degrees and was unable to make myself move beyond it. I had spent so much time worrying about the possibility of dislocating my new hip that it took some time for my brain to process the fact that I was allowed to move more freely, and would not endanger my hip by doing so.

I was functioning reasonably well on my cane but could not walk long distances. My pain and swelling had decreased although both continued to be problematic. I stopped my last dose of Percocet and started outpatient physiotherapy at the hospital at the end of July. My new physiotherapist put me in a contraption called a therma press, which was a device that was strapped to my leg and applied slow but continuous pressure. The therma press felt like it was massaging my leg and its purpose was to reduce the remainder of my swelling. It worked fairly well and within a couple of weeks, both legs were *almost* of equal size again.

The new physio also reevaluated my exercises. She discontinued a number of exercises that were no longer necessary, such as the ankle pumps and the gluteal squeezes. And she added new ones like standing on my operated leg by itself, and lying on my back with my knees up and raising my buttocks in the air. The latter is called "bridging." We also worked on bending my knee towards my chest while I was lying down and while I was seated on the side of the bed. After a few weeks, I began to lie on my nonoperated side and practiced lifting my operated leg up towards the ceiling. My dislike of physiotherapy was directly correlated to the amount of pain that I had; by this time, the pain had diminished considerably and so had my loathing.

TIME SURE DOES FLY WHEN YOU'RE HAVING FUN

Four months after my hip surgery, I had mixed feelings about my progress. On one hand, it was a miracle because I was walking about a mile and a half a day, according to my new and accurate pedometer. That was a mile and a half starting from the time that I got up in the morning until the time that I went to bed at night. I could not walk one and a half miles all at one time yet. At that point, I could walk about one-half of a mile or three-quarters of a mile at once. I was not limited by hip pain but rather by soreness and achiness in my leg muscles and my back.

On the other hand, I was not prepared for such a lengthy recovery and was still feeling frustrated about that. Also, I had to be careful about beginning any new exercises because frequently an exercise or a new sitting position would give me pain for days. I learned to bend over to pick up objects on the floor without my reacher and made a concerted effort to put on my socks without the sock aid. At first, it seemed as though I had a better chance of watching a spaceship land in my backyard than of being able to put on my socks and lace shoes that tied any time in the foreseeable future. Eventually, the soreness diminished while I was performing those tasks. I still remember the day that I was able to get my underwear, my pants, and both my socks on without the aid of a reacher or a sock aid. I felt deliriously happy!

TURNING THE CORNER

One summer day, my friend and I were sitting at an outdoor cafe downtown on Bank Street. I announced that I had seen an ad in the Ottawa Citizen newspaper saying that one of my favorite bands, Matchbox Twenty, was going to be playing at the Corel Centre on October the 6th. "Damn," I lamented. "I'm so tired of missing these concerts!" "So, let's go," she replied. She suggested that we arrive at the concert after the first band had started to play in order to avoid the crowds. I could also arrange for wheelchair assistance in advance. I was doing pretty well on the stairs but I could only navigate stairs that had rails. The Corel Centre had a long series of steps that were wide and deep and did not have a rail. "OK. Let's do it!" I heard myself say. It was then that I knew that I had turned a significant corner in my recovery and was well on my way back to normalcy.

Right after I called Ticketmaster, the Ottawa Citizen ran a front-page article about adults who refused to act their age. Apparently, these immature creatures were dying their hair purple, sporting tattoos and going to rock concerts instead of staying at home to tuck in the grandchildren or enjoying a sensible evening out at the symphony. I decided that buying the tickets for Matchbox Twenty was not enough. I went out and bought a short-sleeved black T-shirt that said "ROCKER" in gold lame. Born-again Rocker was more like it since I hadn't been to a major rock concert at a stadium in over 20 years!

Meanwhile, I was making plans to resume volunteer work in the psychology department at Carleton University and to take a trip out to Winnipeg to see the "younger" friend of my late grandparents, who would be turning 101 at the end of October. If I wanted to see him, the time was now or never.

Six months after my hip replacement, my walking was good and the cane was long gone. I had very little pain or discomfort in my joint unless I was doing strenuous exercises, but my muscles continued to ache with exertion. I took up miniature golf at an indoor arcade and quickly became addicted to the sport, despite the fact that my score was well above the par. The glow in the dark arcade was so much fun that I didn't care how badly I performed, and the music was sufficiently loud that no one noticed when I sang along off key. Walking around the small golf course was not a problem but reaching down to pick up the ball 17 times was an effort. Initially, I brought my reacher with me but I don't use it anymore.

The spaceship had landed! Finally, I could bend all the way down to put on my socks and tie my shoes. However, my hip felt sore for a few minutes after I got my shoes on. I could not get down into the bathtub — well, I was sure that I could get *into* the tub but I had no guarantee that I could get out! I still took stairs one at a time rather than putting one foot after the other, as my operated leg did not seem strong enough to support me on the stairs. I also backed into my car when I got into the driver's seat instead of standing on my left leg and getting in normally.

THE MATCHSTICK BOYS

As my older nephew would say, Matchbox Twenty was "phat." Except that my nephew wouldn't say that about the Matchstick

Boys because they're not his kind of band. He's a DJ and plays a wide variety of electronic music. He likes techno and hip-hop; Aunt Sigrid's rock and roll just doesn't do it for him. The staff at the Corel Centre was gracious and accommodating. One man helped to arrange "transportation" for me and another escorted me to my seat in the dreaded wheelchair. I was embarrassed to be at a rock concert in a wheelchair, but my friend reassured me that lead singer and major heartthrob, Rob Thomas, would not ridicule me if he saw me waving at him from my portable seat. My friend and I had a fantastic time at the concert. I even stood up and sang along with the band for the last few numbers. In fact, I almost started dancing and my friend shouted, "Go girl!" But it was hard to hear her since we were both wearing earplugs. We may have been born-again rockers but we had been resurrected with a lower noise threshold than we had had in our thirties.

WINNIPEG

My trip to Winnipeg was wonderful. My 101-year-old friend and I had never met before. We had just corresponded on e-mail. We got along famously and he threw a big party on behalf of my mother and me. I invited some friends and relatives and everyone had a ball.

It was the first time that I had traveled in years and I hardly thought about my hip, except that I could not get into the pool at the hotel because the steps leading down to the water were too steep. Instead of swimming, I lounged in the whirlpool, which had been conveniently designed with steps down into the tub and had a large metal rail in the center. Once again, I used a wheelchair in the airport since the lines to check in were very long. I could not stand in line for 20 to 30 minutes and walk a considerable distance at the same time. Nor was I able to drag my carry-on luggage on the escalators. Next trip! My new hip set off the metal detectors at the airport. Fortunately, I was prepared for this problem and had warned airport security in advance. I sent my surgeon a postcard from Winnipeg expressing my gratitude to him. Without his help, I would never have made the trip.

Sigrid Macdonald

"I WAS SO MUCH OLDER THEN. I'M YOUNGER THAN THAT NOW."

The Byrds

It has been more than one year since my surgery. Truly, I feel like a whole new person. The hip replacement has taken 20 years off my life. If only I could stabilize my blood sugar and manage my fibromyalgia better, I would feel like Wonder Woman! I was discharged from physiotherapy seven months after the operation but I continue to exercise on a regular basis. Usually, I walk between two to three miles a day. In February, I got lost walking in my brother's neighborhood in Florida and had to walk 2.75 miles to get back to his house. That day I walked more than five miles altogether, without any discomfort in my new hip. That is the longest distance that I have been able to walk since my car accident.

My excursions at The Putting Edge, my indoor mini golf course, no longer seem like exercise; golfing just feels like fun. I love talking to the young, helpful manager who works there, and to his staff. Playing 18 holes is easy for me now and sometimes, I play 36, but my hip feels sore for a few hours after I've bent down 34 times to pick up the ball. Good thing that the final ball is automatically retrieved. My score has dropped 25 points since I started golfing and I am now performing below the par. Also, I am trying to qualify for a tournament at the golf course — "trying" is the operative word here! — but I still sing along to the music off key.

I joined a gym and have been working out on a stationary bicycle, which I enjoy very much. I plan to take up swimming again, although the prospect of removing my clothes makes me shiver in the winter. Swimming outside in a pool, a lake, or the ocean is much more appealing to me than swimming indoors. I don't look like Jane Fonda yet but my Jello thighs have firmed up considerably, and I have built back muscle mass in my operated leg.

I plan to exercise forever. No doubt my inactivity during the 1990s contributed to the collapse of my hip joint. The stronger the muscles are in my legs, the better my new hip will be supported and protected. Given the choice between having a license to be a couch potato versus forced physical activity, it's no contest. I'll take the activity any day.

My hip functions well now but it doesn't feel entirely normal, and the joint is not completely pain-free. It still hurts sometimes and occasionally, I have a dull throbbing ache around the incision. The swelling in my left knee never completely disappeared. I have significantly more pain in that knee since the THR, probably because it was arthritic to begin with, and I fear that I will need to have it replaced in the future. Nonetheless, I'd say that my hip pain postoperatively has decreased by at least 90 percent. I can also do some things now that I thought that I would never be able to do again, such as sitting on the grass or on the floor of my room.

I do have certain limitations. Walking is easy but climbing stairs is more difficult. I am able to take the stairs normally one after another. However, my left leg still feels weak and I rely on stairs with railings. I use pillows in my den and avoid sitting on low chairs when I'm out in public, but I no longer carry pillows with me to the movies or restaurants. I sleep with a pillow between my legs, despite the fact that my surgeon has assured me that this is unnecessary, because I roll over during the night and am afraid that I may inadvertently cross my legs in my sleep. I continue to back into my car most of the time due to weakness in my muscles. Occasionally, I use my reacher to grab objects on the floor but I don't do that very often.

In many respects, my hip seems to be better than the rest of me. In fact, I can't keep up with my new hip! It wants to move faster and farther than my chronically fatigued body can tolerate. Soon, I will be able to wear more feminine shoes instead of spending my life in sneakers. I can't wait to be able to wear my black pumps with the little red dress that has been sitting at the back of my closet.

Several years ago, a friend of mine was walking me to my car at Carleton University. She noticed the disabled sticker on my dashboard. "Look," she exclaimed. "Your sticker is going to expire in the year 2000. That means that you won't be handicapped in the new millennium!" Her prophecy took a few more years to materialize but I am finally parking in the non-handicapped spaces, and walking to the mall and the library from the parking lot like everyone else.

8

The Experience of Other Total Hippers

Recovery from a total hip replacement is a highly individual experience. Many people recover quickly whereas others are slow to resume normal functioning, or have complications along the way. Before you run to the telephone to cancel your date for surgery, fearing that it may be as hard as mine, remember the old Internet acronym: Your Mileage May Vary," (YMMV.) This means that your experience may be entirely different from mine.

Many factors are involved in the recovery process, such as an individual's age, general state of health, quality of bone, muscle tone, and the surgeon's expertise. The basic rule of thumb is that the patient spends five to seven days in the hospital. Post-op physiotherapy initially involves home visits, followed by a progression to an outpatient clinic. Patients whose hips have been cemented may feel steadier on their feet than those who have had the uncemented procedure. People with a cemented prosthesis usually spend about six weeks on crutches or a walker before they graduate to a cane. The uncemented prosthesis often requires more time to heal as patients move from partial to full weight bearing. The recipient will spend at least eight weeks on crutches or a walker. In either case, the books that I read stated that most people who have had total hip replacements dispense with their canes and walk without assistance by the third month postoperatively. But my physiotherapist said that many people continue to use a cane for six to twelve months after surgery, depending on their particular circumstances.

Heal Your Hips: How to Prevent Hip Surgery — and What to Do If You Need It, by Robert Klapper and Lynda Huey, discusses hip surgery although the real goal of the book is to prevent the need for the operation. Despite the excellent advice in this book, Klapper and Huey do seem to minimize hip replacements. They say that the need for pain medication is frequently gone within nine to ten days, and that within two weeks postoperatively, most patients start on crutches and slowly wean themselves on to one crutch. "By the end of six weeks, you should be able to walk without assistive devices and within six to eight weeks you can generally play golf by now," Klapper and Huey assert. No wonder I was discouraged when I was just getting off my walker ten weeks after surgery!

Irwin Silber, author of *A Patient's Guide to Knee and Hip Replacement: Everything You Need to Know* and a professional journalist, had three of his own joints replaced. This included surgery on both knees and his left hip. Today he walks without a cane, rides a bicycle, plays tennis, and otherwise leads a normal life. Silber seems to have a good understanding of the variability of the time that it takes to recover from hip surgery. He states that much of the success of a joint replacement depends on the patient's expectations. Silber also notes that not everyone is free of pain following the operation. He declares that there may be an "80% reduction in pain," and some residual restrictions postoperatively in terms of range of motion and flexibility. According to Silber, the prosthesis may never feel like a normal hip. However, most people will have an improvement in the quality of their lives following a THR.

The key words in the aforementioned comments about total hip replacements are "most," "generally," and "usually." Clearly, I did not experience a swift and painless recovery, and I did not throw away my cane until four months after the surgery.

This chapter is devoted to the discussion of other people's total hip experiences. I have interviewed ten individuals whose recoveries varied from being speedy and simple to lengthy and complicated. The majority needed surgery because they had osteoarthritis. Some had other disorders, such as congenital hip displacement or avascular necrosis, which is a loss of blood supply to the head of the femur. My group is not a representative sample. The average mean age of my group was 58 years old at the time of their surgery, whereas the American Academy of Orthopaedic Surgeons states that the average age of people undergoing a total hip replacement is 69.

Many of the interviewees wrote to me after they read my web site or responded to messages that I posted on support groups for arthritis and joint replacements. Two people are friends of my family. One individual chose to have his hip resurfaced rather than to have a total hip replacement. Resurfacing involves reshaping rather than replacing the head of the femur and is examined in more detail in the section entitled "Michael."

THELMA

Thelma Lubkin is a 62-year-old computer programmer from Wisconsin, who compared her recovery from a THR to having a "bad cold." Her hip joint deteriorated as the result of a bicycle accident in 1974 when she broke her femur one inch below the hip. This was repaired using a steel pin, which was removed one year later. In 1992, Thelma broke the ball of her hip with yet another accident caused by an unexpected encounter with black ice. Her hip was repaired with a Richards screw, "a new permanent feature of my anatomy," as Thelma describes it. She had seven trouble-free years with the Richards screw in place before her hip started to deteriorate, following a third and hopefully, final injury on the bicycle in 2002. This time, both she and her husband, Eli, were hurt. At first, Thelma did not realize the damage that had been done to her hip since her husband's injuries were more apparent than hers, and she felt more pain in her collarbone and the rotator cuffs in both shoulders than in her hip joint.

According to Thelma, "My daughter came home from California to nurse her reckless parents. She documents that at the beginning of her visit, I had a sore collarbone but was otherwise getting around fine. By the time she left about three weeks later, I had lost range of motion in both shoulders. I couldn't get on the tandem without my husband waiting patiently for me somehow, via painful contortions, to climb into the seat. I couldn't even pull the heavy quilt in my bed around freely."

By the time that Thelma's daughter returned to California in late October, Thelma knew that she needed to consult with an orthopedic surgeon. Her first appointment was in December with the doctor who had installed her Richards screw. Unfortunately, he did not perform hip replacements so he referred her to one of his office mates, who was "one of the top three orthopedists in the area for that procedure." After that, Thelma sought a second opinion and decided to go with a surgeon whom she saw in January of 2003. She chose this man because she was very pleased "with his resume, everything from his large practice in joint replacements to active research work, and an impressive list of published papers. I was impressed by his eagerness to explain what he would do at whatever technical level he felt he could push you to — no 'I'm the doctor, you don't need to know anything else' attitude here. I appreciated his easy going friendliness…and I liked the fact that he used an anterior approach in the surgery, a procedure that has a much lower dislocation rate than the usual posterior approach."

Thelma had her surgery in March of 2003 and had very little pain afterwards. In fact, she never took so much as a Tylenol in the hospital, and had difficulty convincing the nurses that she did not need any medication for pain. Six weeks after the operation, Thelma arrived at her doctor appointment using two crutches. She left the office with permission to walk without them, and walked from there to a custard stand one mile away using a single crutch. Thelma celebrated her new freedom with an ice cream cone, took a bus home and rode 13 miles on the tandem that afternoon. Two weeks later, she was walking unassisted. "That six week post-op appointment was the turning point after which I resumed full activity. I'm still recovering in the sense that my confidence in the hip's solidity keeps getting reinforced," Thelma explains.

Sometimes, Thelma feels twinges of pain when she makes certain twisting motions, on steep stairs or bicycling uphill. However, in general, she is doing extremely well and believes that her new hip will outlast the rest of her. She does not avoid any particular positions. In fact, she feels so confident that she will tuck her left leg up under her rear end and sit that way, even though her THR is on the left side. Thelma not only crosses her legs, but sometimes she will "double cross her legs" by putting one leg over the other and then the other one coming part way over again. "I've spent so much of my life in pretzel positions that I'm willing to take my chances," Thelma declares.

"The surgery was the complete success that I had expected. After all, I had a surgeon, Dr. J.B. Stiehl, who was not only a technical master and an active contributor to the development of joint replacement procedures, but also a man with a fine bedside manner and an eagerness to give us as much information as we could absorb about the procedure."

You can read more about Thelma's satisfaction with her new hip in the article, "Notes on my Total Hip Replacement" on her web site at http://www.armory.com/~mom/THR.html.

ARLETTE

Another woman whose recovery was relatively fast and uncomplicated is Arlette Hill. Arlette is 71 years old, retired and living in upstate New York. Her hip joint deteriorated as a result of osteoarthritis, which she attributes to a horseback riding accident in the early 1980s. At that time, she fractured her ankle. This did not interfere with her life significantly, but she did have pain in her knee at times and developed a limp when she was tired. Four years ago, the pain in Arlette's knee became much worse and then traveled to her hip. Her orthopedic surgeon does not believe that the injury to her ankle caused the problem in her hip, but Arlette disagrees.

"My doctor insists the hip came first. It got to the point where I'd have to use two canes to walk and the pain became unbearable. This is when my doctor sent me to an orthopedic surgeon, who took one look at my x-rays and said, 'surgery now or pain forever'. I had the surgery on July 9th, 2003, three weeks after the diagnosis. For three days after the surgery, it was very painful to get in and out of bed. I spent three days on the surgical floor and seven days on the rehab floor. By the time I was discharged, I could pretty well function by myself (I live alone.) I used a walker for three weeks, then a cane for three months. I don't have pain in my hip, just discomfort at times. I do not have pain in the other hip, but I do have stiffness and sometimes pain in my knee and I feel it may be the first stage, or the last depending on which way you look at it. I am more concerned about having to have the other hip done than the new one failing."

GILLIAN

Gillian Smith is 65 years old, retired and living outside of London in the United Kingdom. She had both hips replaced in 1993, one in June and the second in October. This was followed by a total knee replacement in 2001; another knee replacement is scheduled for 2004. Gill has a long family history of osteoarthritis. Her father had both hips replaced and so did his sister. Gillian's sister had a knee, a hip and two shoulder replacements. She is currently waiting for surgery on her other knee and her hip. And Gillian's daughter, who is only 32, is starting to have trouble with both her hip and her knee.

Gillian's arthritis began with an injury that she sustained as a teenager. "I had two sprained knees when I was 16, which didn't get proper medical care. Over the years my hips started to deteriorate. By the time I got to the age of 50, I was in a lot of pain and found it difficult to walk long distances. I went to my doctor several times. Although he said I had some wear on the hip joints, there wasn't enough wear to worry about. I carried on for a few more years, but my life was a strain. I was a dining room manager at a local golf course and was on my feet most of the day. Even the simplest of jobs was a torture to do. I decided to go to another doctor within the same practice. She took one look at the way I was walking and immediately referred me to an orthopaedic surgeon. I had to wait a long time to see him and when I eventually was ushered into his room, he shook his head saying, "You are too young for this operation."

The doctor relented and put Gillian on his waiting list for hip surgery sometime during 1992 or 1993. She had the first hip done in June at the age of 55. Gill was in the hospital for nine days, went home on crutches and started to work again in a reduced capacity three weeks after the operation. "When the surgeon came to see me the day after I had my hip done, I immediately said, 'When can I have the next one done?' He said he would get me on the list straight away. I finally got the second replacement in October of the same year."

Gillian's first hip replacement went well, although she had extreme pain on the day after the operation. However, she has a high tolerance for pain and was out of bed the following day on crutches. Three days later, Gill graduated to walking sticks. Six weeks post-op, she managed without her canes on many occasions, but did not dispense with them entirely until three months after the replacement.

The second hip replacement occurred the following October. It also went well and she recovered quickly, but because the national health system was afraid of leaving their beds empty, Gillian was "stuck" in the hospital for three weeks before they would let her out. She refers to this practice as "bed warming." Eight weeks after the operation, Gill returned to work and since that time, she has continued to use a cane. Occasionally, she has pain in her hips, depending on her activities, but she tries to stay as active as possible. She prefers to sit on a high chair since she has some difficulty getting up from a low chair.

"Because my hips were so bad, they put a strain on my knees. I had a knee replacement two years ago and that went very well. I was in hospital for eight days, used two sticks when I came out of hospital, and went down to one stick a few weeks later. I was going to have the other knee done a few weeks ago, but because I have heart problems now, they would not operate until I had further tests done on my heart. My ankles have started giving way, but I don't think the outlook for ankle replacement is very good at present. I am also starting to have trouble with the shoulder joints and the finger joints. So far my hips have lasted about 10 years. Hopefully I will have at least another five to 10 years with them."

Gillian's heart tests were performed during the winter of 2004 and she is currently waiting for her knee replacement.

RALPH

Ralph Stevens was a general manager for a welding supply company. He is 51 years old and is currently retired on disability, living in Westfield, New Brunswick, Canada. He was born with hip displacement, which was not repaired until 1963 when he was eleven years old. "The repair back then was at best a patch job of plastic surgery. After the surgery in 1963, although there was not a lot of pain, the joint never felt right and I had very little movement of the hip joint. I began to have major problems around 1980 and had hip pain on a constant basis. The joint deteriorated to the point by 1988 that I could no longer walk on it."

According to Ralph's wife, Patty, Ralph has a high pain threshold. He always had some degree of pain and was limited in his activities, but he tolerated this for many years. Then there came a time when the pain was unbearable and something had to be done. Medication did not provide adequate relief.

"There was not a doctor in Saint John at the time that felt comfortable performing a hip replacement in Ralph's case," Patty told me. "One doctor actually told him there was nothing that could be done. A new orthopaedic doctor came to town and recommended a specialist in Moncton, N.B. It was in Moncton where the operation was done. From a spouse's view, it was difficult trying to be in two places at once, not to mention traveling on snowy roads. It was wintertime and we had two small children, one in kindergarten and one in grade three. Moncton is approximately 100 miles from our home."

"The orthopaedic surgeon gave me two options: a total hip replacement or hip fusion," Ralph says. "A hip fusion would have meant that I would have lost all movement in the joint and that would have been permanent, with no option in the future for any repair or revision. It was decided that a total hip replacement was the best option. I waited around eight months to have the surgery performed, and it was done in November of 1989 at the age of 37. Due to the very poor condition of my hip joint, the surgeon had to do an extensive bone graft, so that he had something to anchor the new socket to. I spent two weeks in the hospital. The pain, although quite severe after the surgery, was well managed by at least six injections of morphine a day. In retrospect, the pain from the removal of bone tissue for the bone graft, which was taken from the back of my pelvis, was more severe."

"When discharged from the hospital I used crutches, with no weight bearing on the hip for eight weeks. I then moved on to a cane, which I still use. It took about six to eight months to return to the point of pre-surgery," Ralph informed me. "I had a revision of the hip in May of 2001, a period of twelve years on the original. The liner in the socket had worn and pieces were coming off, and causing a great deal of pain and discomfort. The liner was replaced and a new head was also installed. I only spent five days in hospital and it was a much easier surgery to deal with. Was able to weight bear the next day!"

83

"I should explain that because my hip was not repaired at birth, as it should have been, I have a number of other problems. My right leg is approximately two inches shorter than my left. In my early years, I walked with a severe gait and this has resulted in spine and neck problems. I had a fusion on my neck in 1996 to C4, C5, and C6 disks. I am not able to walk any sort of distance, and must use a wheelchair, although I still manage to get around the house with my cane. I am presently waiting to see if I will need further surgery on my neck, as I am having some major problems again."

Despite the complexity of Ralph's situation, the severe pain that he endured after his primary hip replacement, and the fact that he must rely on a wheelchair most of the time now outside of his house, Ralph said unequivocally that he was glad that he had the two THRs. Even though he is not that active physically, the joint is free of pain, which is a relief to him. Unfortunately, the post of the hip replacement — the point at which it is cemented into the existing bone — has shown small signs of loosening. If this has to be repaired, the procedure may be as difficult as having another total hip replacement. Since Ralph does not walk that much, he hopes that the hip will last a few more years. Revision hip surgeries are not always as successful as the primary replacement and Ralph has already had one revision.

LUCY

Lucy A. Hoover is a 55-year-old executive assistant for an aviation company in Van Nuys, California. She had polio as a small child and was born with a hereditary defect in her hip. This was aggravated by a bicycle accident, which occurred when she was approximately 30 years old. When her hip joint began to deteriorate, first her doctor thought that a pinched nerve in her lower back was causing her discomfort. Consequently, she was treated with physical therapy for about five months. During that time, her pain and discomfort fluctuated.

Then one morning, Lucy couldn't get out of bed. She went to a doctor who specialized in pain management, and he took an x-ray of her hip. Her cartilage had deteriorated and she was grinding bone on bone. Two and a half months later, in May of 2001, Lucy had a total hip replacement.

"I wanted to wait a little longer, but the pain was unbearable and I worked full time up to the day of my surgery. I decided to have the surgery because I couldn't function in my everyday routine. It was painful sitting down, going back to a standing position, walking, going up and down stairs and getting in and out of a car. When I got home at night after work, I would basically stand until I could lie down and go to bed."

"I mostly remember having pain just the first couple of days after surgery. I am not able to tolerate painkillers, so by the third day I was only on Tylenol. On the third day, I was also moved to a Rehab Center adjacent to the hospital. I stayed there for six days. I would experience pain as I was trying to walk and of course, doing exercises. Around six days after surgery, I stopped using a walker and started using crutches. I had used crutches before and was more comfortable using them. They actually forced me to walk better. By the third week, I started using a cane and was walking two miles a day. After that, I sometimes used one crutch if I was in a crowd for protection. I stopped using any assistive devices when I returned to work at six weeks."

Lucy went to physical therapy for five months after her surgery. She started driving a car three weeks after the operation but she drove "very carefully." At that time, Lucy began hydrotherapy. She worked out in the water and on land, and continued to follow the 90 degree precautions. A full recovery from the surgery did not occur until somewhere between nine to twelve months postoperatively. Now, "the only lingering aggravation that I have is a burning in my hip from sitting too long, or sitting in a chair that isn't at a 90 degree angle, or sitting and leaning forward."

Like most of the people that I interviewed, Lucy was pleased with the results of her surgery. But she stated that her recovery took longer than she had anticipated. "I thought that because I was younger than most, 55 years old, that I would just pop back. I have always been very athletic and in good shape. So, I thought that combination would help. It's very possible that it did, however, I didn't think it was going to be quite as difficult as it was."

Lucy has returned to all of her normal activities except jogging and tennis, but she has slowed down. Lucy avoids moving too quickly and pays more attention when she walks since she has tripped a couple of times. This has resulted in minor discomfort for a week or so. Lucy does not want to have revision surgery, therefore, she is "trying to remain conservative" and not to wear her implant down.

GERARD

53-year old Gerard T. Kelly is a business manager in Canfield, Ohio. He was a physical education major in college and ran on a regular basis from 1973 until 1988. Gerard ran an average of more than 40 miles per week. He ran in six marathons and was also an avid backpacker from 1978 through 1991. He would travel anywhere from 14 miles on a weekend trip up to 600 miles on a 60-day trip.

Gerard's arthritic pain began sometime in 1993. At that time, his work demands diminished and he had two young daughters, which decreased his ability to stay physically active. This resulted in a weight gain of approximately 60 pounds. In 1997, he began to experience daily pain and the inability to sleep through the night. By 2000, at the age of 50, Gerard "could not walk up steps without pulling on a hand rail." He had developed a visible limp and complained to his family doctor. X-rays showed that the joint space in both hips had significantly deteriorated so that the joint was bone on bone, with bone spurs further limiting his motion. Physical therapy and Celebrex did not alleviate Gerard's discomfort.

By August of 2003, Gerard said, "enough is enough." He arranged to have a THR on his right hip on October 24, 2003. Although the x-rays showed that his left hip had deteriorated more than the right hip, Gerard experienced more pain in the right hip and decided to have it done first. Before the surgery, he spoke to some friends who were occupational therapists. They advised him to take advantage of pain medication postoperatively so that he would always be one step ahead of the pain.

After the operation, Gerard had a difficult time with the anesthesia, which made him throw up. He accepted all of the pain medication that the nurses gave him for the first two days following surgery, even when he was not in pain. "In fact, I felt little pain. And since the surgery, I have NEVER felt pain from the incision or hip joint. I just felt sick a lot the first two days. I walked the day after surgery, but was sick from the meds. Felt like throwing up. Within 48 hours post-op, I was doing laps of the hospital corridor, including steps and getting into and out of a bathtub."

Gerard was impressed with the fact that his surgeon came in to see him at 6:30 a.m. for the first three mornings after the operation. This included a Saturday, Sunday and Monday morning. His occupational therapists were very helpful and instructive and his family doctor also went to see him in the hospital. Three days after the surgery, Gerard was sent home. He had a visiting nurse and physiotherapist twice a week for the first three weeks. He used a walker for three weeks and transferred briefly on to a cane for two days, which he referred to as a "waste of money," since he was able to walk without any assistance after that.

Less than a month after the surgery, Gerard returned to his desk job and started driving the car. He drove to Philadelphia and back from Ohio over the Thanksgiving holidays, during week five post-op. The trip was 380 miles each way and he did all of the driving "without incident." Gerard "walked gingerly" until week five; by week six, he was "walking without thinking about walking," which was "a nice feeling."

When I interviewed Gerard, it had only been eight weeks since his surgery. He said that he was "feeling great" except that he may have pushed himself too hard by resuming weight lifting and trying military presses, which gave him a bit of groin pain in the new hip. He was still adhering to the precautions including the use of a raised toilet seat and assistive devices for putting on his socks and shoes.

Gerard had an extremely fast recovery. He was also given a ceramic hip. "My surgeon felt that my (relatively) young age (53) necessitated a low wear replacement. I know that the ceramic has been knocked, but the medical industry feels the major issues against it have been resolved." The FDA only approved the ceramic hip in February of 2003. There is some controversy surrounding its use, which is discussed in greater detail in chapter 10, but when ceramic hips work well, they may last a lifetime.

"My experience has been great. The pain is minimal; I'd say 10% of what I had expected. I've been active all these years, even through the arthritic pain, and feel that has been beneficial to the recovery process (note — don't try sitting military presses!") Prior to surgery, the surgeon said: "When you get home and want something, don't ask for it, get up and get it." Gerard plans to have his left hip replaced late next summer. His advice for people who are contemplating hip surgery? "Don't wait! Get it done now!"

JOHN

John Parke is a 46-year-old sales manager for E & J Gallo Winery in California. He had his right hip replaced three years ago at the age of 43. John has avascular necrosis, otherwise known as osteonecrosis. This disease causes a temporary or permanent loss of blood supply to the bones. Without blood, the bone tissue dies and causes the bone to collapse. If the damaged bone is near a joint, it may lead to the collapse of the joint surface.

"Before the surgery, I was moving like an old man," John declares. He spent seven or eight days in the hospital and found the first two days postoperatively to be painful and difficult. "It was just terrible," he said. John donated two units of his own blood, which he did not need. However, he did take iron orally for one month following the surgery. He had a spinal anesthesia and took morphine injections for pain. John was given anti-embolism stockings right away and did not experience any complications, nor did he have any difficulty following the precautions.

After he left the hospital, John slept downstairs on the first floor of his house in a hospital bed for two weeks. He spent approximately six weeks on crutches and three months post-op, he was back to playing golf. After the surgery, John returned to playing doubles tennis, both downhill and cross-country skiing, and ice skating. He realized that some of these sports may be dangerous for his new hip if he were to fall, but he loved those activities and was willing to take that risk.

John said that he has regained approximately 80 percent of his former mobility. His new hip does not feel entirely normal but he considers the operation to have been a success, and is extremely grateful to be active once again. John is aware of his prosthesis and said that he feels almost as though he is "parenting the thing."

Unfortunately, his left hip gave out on him recently and he just had another THR in March of 2004. He had a great deal of confidence in his team of doctors, and was not surprised that the second surgery went as well as the first. However, since John's second hip replacement, he has been reconsidering his views on downhill skiing and may just hang up his skis for good. The prospect makes him sad but he does not wish to repeat the hip operation anytime in the near future.

Zimmer, the same company that made the acetabular component of my implant, made John's prosthesis. Our implants are composed of crosslinked polyethylene, which is more durable than regular polyethylene. John hopes that his new hips will last 10 to 20 years.

SUZANNE

Suzanne Carlos is a 73-year-old woman living in Ottawa, Ontario. She used to work for the government in the department of Industry, Trade and Commerce, and taught at a college in Montreal. Suzanne has a long history of arthritic pain that dates back almost 50 years.

For years, Suzanne did not realize that some of the pain that she felt in her back was coming from her hip. She tried acupuncture and chiropractic, to no avail, and finally saw an orthopedist that specialized in backs. Despite the fact that Suzanne had arthritis in her back, the doctor told her it was not her back that was the primary problem, but rather her hip. He referred her to a surgeon who specialized in hip replacements. "He sends me his backs and I send him my hips," the doctor told Suzanne.

The new surgeon said that Suzanne needed a total hip replacement. She waited eight to nine months for the surgery and was in quite a bit of pain and discomfort during this time. To complicate matters, Suzanne's husband, Don, had a stroke and spent a considerable amount of time in a wheelchair. He relied on Suzanne to care for him; therefore, it was difficult for both of them when Suzanne's hip deteriorated.

Immediately after the surgery, Suzanne felt "wonderful." Her long-standing pain was gone and she was extremely relieved. She was also pleased to discover that she had been a bone donor. Her surgeon kept a good piece of bone from her hip joint and put it in a bone bank for people who need bone grafts. It took several months for Suzanne's blood tests to be approved by the bone bank. She spent about a week in the hospital and two weeks in a convalescent center afterwards with her husband before they were able to return home.

At home, Suzanne began to experience frustration with her inability to drive. "I was so disappointed during this time," she says. She relied on a walker for about six weeks and transferred on to a cane, which she used for some time. Now she walks without assistance unless she is going out in the wintertime or is very tired, in which case she will use her cane.

Suzanne is free of pain in her hip but continues to experience discomfort in her back. Physiotherapy has helped her with the latter and she has resumed all of her normal activities.

MICHAEL

63-year-old Michael Bentley is retired and living in Denmark. He attributes the arthritic deterioration of his right hip to wear and tear caused by many years of one sided work involved in tire fitting. "The first pain began late in 2001 and rapidly made normal activities very difficult. This made me decide to find a surgical solution."

Michael could have had a conventional hip replacement but instead he decided to go to Belgium in June of 2003 to have his hip resurfaced. Resurfacing was introduced in 1991 by Corin Medical. There are two major distinctions between a traditional THR and a resurfaced hip. The first difference is that both parts of the prosthesis are made from metal, which makes it last much longer than the traditional metal on plastic implant. The second difference is that the head of the femur is simply reshaped and "resurfaced," rather than removed. The preservation of the femoral head results in less bone loss, making revision surgery much easier. So far, Corin Medical claims that hip resurfacing has a good success rate, particularly on younger patients, but its long-term performance has yet to be seen.

In addition, many doctors are not familiar with resurfacing or are not qualified to perform the surgery. Resurfacing is not suitable for all patients; some types of arthritis lead to significant deformity of either the head of the femur or the acetabulum. This may preclude the option of hip resurfacing.

Hip resurfacing results in fewer precautions to follow compared to a traditional THR. "Although still quite new, the success rate for resurfacing does seem to be better than for THR," Michael says. Michael was not fitted with the Corin model but rather with the Birmingham Hip Replacement, manufactured in Birmingham, England by Mid Mec Technologies. "My surgeon has now done more than 1000 resurfacings to date, and as far as I know, he has only had three failures. If it does fail, I can still have a THR at a future date."

"The restrictions normally associated with THRs do not apply, and the only ones regularly mentioned for resurfacing are no bungee jumping or parachuting. I can cross my legs without any problem, and haven't been warned against it. Dislocation with resurfacing is virtually unheard of due to retaining the original femur head. I personally do not engage in any sports, but many people do take up their previous sports. A man who was in Belgium with me from Arizona, is now back to competing in rodeos," Michael exclaims.

Michael waited two months for the surgery and experienced severe muscle pain for several days afterwards. "I was given painkillers consisting of paracetemol (similar to acetaminophen) and codeine, and I needed to continue with this medication for about ten days. I used two crutches the first few days, but was able to manage with one after about two weeks, and stopped using crutches altogether after two months."

"I was fully recovered from the surgery, i.e. wound healed, swelling subsided and bruising gone, about two weeks after surgery. I drove at nine days after the operation (different rules apply to resurfacing,) but other everyday activities took rather longer, more like a month." Seven months after the surgery, Michael experienced some "nasty pains in the operated hip area," which have since passed. These were investigated with x-rays and blood tests, and much to his relief, he did not have an infection. Michael's surgeon in Belgium said that this sort of thing could happen during the first year postoperatively and could "be brought on by a change in activity levels, or even the weather!" However, the prosthesis is sitting perfectly, which was a big relief to him.

Michael's muscles "are still a long way from being back to normal. Also, in the scar area (12" long,) I experience a moderate lack of sensation, probably due to nerve damage." He has returned to his normal activities but does tend to protect his hip to a certain degree, "for example, when going up steps, always favouring the un-operated leg." His worries for the future concern the possibility of infection. In general, Michael says that he is "a thousand times better than I had become immediately prior to surgery, and basically my life has returned to what it was before."

You can learn more about hip resurfacing in the fascinating, well researched book called *Hip Replacement or Hip Resurfacing: A Story of Choices* by Peggy Gabriel. Gabriel was scheduled to have both hips replaced but decided against the THRs after she learned about the limitations that she would have postoperatively, which would have interfered with her career as a Pilates Instructor. Instead, she went to Belgium in 2002 to have her hips resurfaced. Gabriel wrote an account of her own experience, including her struggle with her insurance company. She also included stories of other people's experiences with hip resurfacing, as well as useful facts and information about this alternative to the traditional hip replacement.

EDWARD

Edward Marshall is a pseudonym for a retired sales and marketing representative. He is 68 years old, lives in Arizona and had his right hip replaced with a metal-on-metal prosthesis in October of 2000. His arthritic hip deteriorated quickly and went from giving him occasional discomfort to a near crippling level of pain within eight months. "For the last six months before surgery, day to day activities were just tolerable; fun activities (hiking, swimming, playing golf) were impossible. I proceeded with surgery to get back the fun parts of life."

Ed was 64 years old at the time of the surgery. So far, his hip has lasted four years and he expects it to last a lifetime because the prosthesis is composed entirely of metal parts. Not only is metal stronger than polyethylene, but also the use of a polyethylene socket creates plastic debris within the hip over a period of time. This causes the bone to dissolve. When polyethylene is not used, there is no plastic debris. Consequently, the risk of developing bone osteolysis (bone loss) diminishes, as does the need for revision surgery.

Ed only waited eight weeks for the operation. He could have had it done within five to six weeks of making his decision, but postponed the surgery to attend a family wedding. He had a spinal anesthetic. "I had very severe pain the night after the surgery due to a series of muscle spasms in the operated leg. That was brought under control only after added doses of morphine. For the next several days, I was in moderate pain, pretty well controlled by 'patient-controlled analgesia,' or self-administered intravenous doses of morphine. I went home directly from the hospital four days after the surgery, and continued to use narcotic-type painkillers (Vicodin) at decreasing levels over the next three weeks."

"I started walking the day after the surgery with a walker — weight bearing on the operated leg 'as tolerated.' I continued with the walker for three weeks, and then switched to a cane for another two weeks. Walked without assist at about five weeks. I started driving at about three and a half weeks, and that was the start of everyday activities. I was retired at the time, but was okay to return to work at four weeks."

"Today, I am doing fine. I have slightly reduced range of motion, just due to the physical characteristics of the prosthesis. I have occasional minor discomfort — muscle related — not enough to need any pain medication. I play golf two or three times a week and play as well as before the surgery. I'm restricted from all activities that create impact — running, racquetball, tennis, etc. Not much of an issue for me."

Ed has some worries about the long-term consequences of having a metal-on-metal implant, but he doesn't think about it very often.

CONCLUSIONS

The ten people that I interviewed had very different experiences following hip surgery. Many of these individuals had swift recoveries but some took more than six months to fully recover from their THRs. Several people attributed the onset of their arthritis to accidents or sports injuries. Two mentioned receiving poor medical care at the time of their injury, which could have caused or aggravated their arthritis. Others developed osteoarthritis as the result of normal activity or because of a disease such as avascular necrosis. A number of the interviewees had arthritic pain and deterioration in several joints, which necessitated the need for multiple joint replacements. Predictably, the two Canadians waited longer than anyone else for hip surgery.

People defined recovery differently. For example, Lucy returned to work and walked without any assistive devices six weeks postoperatively. However, she did not consider herself to be recovered from her hip surgery until nine to twelve months had passed. On the other hand, Michael considered himself to be completely recovered two weeks after the surgery, despite the fact that he was still using one crutch and his muscles had not returned to normal.

Two of the ten interviewees are still using a cane regularly today, and another requires a cane occasionally. Of these, one man can function on a cane inside his house but needs a wheelchair when he goes out. Revision surgery was only required by one individual; unfortunately, he may still need additional surgery on his hip. The majority of these people had their hips replaced with the standard metal on plastic implants, but two people opted for different materials in their implant, namely ceramic and metal-on-metal. One man had his hip resurfaced instead of having a total hip replacement.

Everyone that I interviewed was pleased that they had the operation, even if they had not been restored to a fully mobile and pain-free state. Many people in the group had done extensive research about hip replacements on their own, and were extremely well informed about the recovery process and the nature of their own implants.

9

Taking Care of a New Hip

REVISION SURGERY

If you have just had a hip replacement, you will want the prosthesis to last as long as possible so that you can avoid or delay a revision. Revisions are more complicated than primary joint replacements and their success rate is not as high. Revisions take much longer to perform because the surgeon has to remove the old implant, which may have been cemented in or have become infected. If the joint is infected, the infection must be treated aggressively before a new prosthesis can be inserted. Sometimes, this involves taking out the patient's hip and leaving a person without a hip for several weeks while they are on intravenous antibiotics.

The bone at the head of the femur may also have deteriorated. This is referred to as osteolysis and is a common cause of failure of the primary joint replacement. Ronald Allen, Victoria Brander and Dr. S. David Stulberg describe bone lysis as the result of the implant materials wearing out over time. This is particularly true of the plastic in the prosthesis, which can break down and create "particles that float around in the hip joint." These particles may erode the bone. M.T. Simon notes that patients with an uncemented prosthesis have a greater incidence of bone lysis five years after the surgery than those with a cemented implant. Sometimes, Richard Villar adds, the bone has degenerated so much that a bone graft is required.

Another reason why hips give out is that the implant itself becomes less secure; this is called "loosening" and is more likely to occur with a cemented prosthesis. Loosening can occur without any symptoms, which is why regular follow-up x-rays are important. Other causes of failure of the artificial joint are hip fractures, dislocations and infections.

Local anesthesia injected into the spine may not be an option during a revision. Some surgeons offer patients a spinal anesthetic but others feel that it is too risky, because the operation takes longer than the first hip replacement. Estimates for the amount of time that it takes to perform a THR vary from ninety minutes to two hours for the first replacement and between three to six hours for revision surgery. The time involved depends on an individual's health, age and the complexity of his or her situation.

People are likely to lose more blood during a revision and the final result is not apt to provide as much security, flexibility, and range of motion as the original hip replacement. M.T. Simon wrote her book *Hip Replacements: What You Need to Know* because her mother had a hip replacement at a young age and required a revision later on in life. Before the second operation, Simon asked the surgeon about the risks involved for her mother. He said that there was a "25 percent likelihood" that her mother would never walk again after the operation. Simon was shocked to receive this news, which was only forthcoming after she repeatedly questioned the man.

There is a greater chance of the surgeon breaking the hip joint or femur during a revision, especially if the joint has been cemented. Some patients may require several revisions during their lifetime. This is especially true if they were under the age of 50 at the time of their original THR. If you have just had a total hip replacement, you will want to do everything that is humanly possible to get the most out of your first hip.

HOW LONG WILL THE IMPLANT LAST?

According to the Orthopedic Institute of the Memorial Medical Center in Springfield, Illinois, "Approximately 90 to 95 percent of hip replacements last 10 years and 80 percent last up to 20 years. The major long-term problem is loosening of the prosthesis." M.T. Simon states that many hip replacements have lasted 20 or even 25 years and are still functioning perfectly well. Most hip patients are elderly when they have their hips replaced and their implants may very well outlive them. However, Richard Villar claims that the average lifespan for a total hip is 10 years and "that is an average, not a guarantee."

Many factors influence the length of time that the artificial joint will last. Obviously, age at the time of the first surgery is important. "The younger the patient, the shorter the hip replacement is likely to last," Villar asserts. He quotes an American study from 1983, which consisted of more than 100 patients under the age of 45. "An average of four and a half years after the procedure, only 76 percent of the replacements were still satisfactory."

If primary total hip replacements are so successful, why would almost one-quarter of the younger people in this study have complaints less than five years after their surgeries? Were they more physically active than the older patients? Did they take more risks? Did they disregard the precautions? Or were the expectations of a 45-year-old different from the expectations of a 75-year-old? Perhaps success was defined differently; to an 80-year-old, success may have meant freedom from pain whereas to a 40-year-old, success might have meant the ability to function normally. Did the younger patients expect the prosthesis to act and feel like a normal hip? A prosthesis is an artificial joint. Some people barely notice their implants and their hips feel completely normal following surgery. Others are always aware that the implant is a foreign object. Having an artificial joint may significantly decrease hip pain and increase mobility, but the hip may continue to ache or throb with exertion, weather, or strenuous activities.

WHY DO IMPLANTS FAIL?

Let's review the most common causes for hip failure in more detail and see what can be done to prevent them. Poor surgical technique, infection, dislocation, loosening, fractures, and osteolysis all have the potential to cause implants to give out prematurely. The specific design of the implant will also influence its longevity, as will the degree of compliance that the patient has exhibited postoperatively by carefully following the precautions, and by doing the physiotherapy exercises on a daily basis.

FINDING THE BEST SURGEON

The single most important variable that will enhance the longevity of your prosthesis is surgical skill and expertise. Choose your surgeon wisely. Make sure that he or she has performed a number of hip replacements, that there is a specially designed orthopedic ward in his hospital and a short-term or geriatric rehabilitation unit, if possible. Pick a surgeon that you are comfortable with, someone you like and respect, who has empathy and provides you with enough time during an office visit. Get a second opinion if you are uneasy with the first surgeon you see, because your relationship with the surgeon may last for many years. You will see him or her frequently after the operation for follow-up visits, and probably once every 12 months after that to make sure that your implant is still in the proper position, and to monitor your progress.

Many people are insured by HMOs, Medicare or by a national health care system that may discourage their right to doctor shop. Orthopedists are in short supply so it may be difficult to find one at all, let alone one that you are crazy about. The search is made harder still when you are in pain and your mobility is limited. But if you can summon the physical energy for this pursuit and the persistence to persuade your insurance company to pay for a second opinion, it will be well worth your while in the long run to be with the surgeon of your choice. The expertise with which the implant is inserted makes a considerable difference to its lifespan, as does the quality of the material, design, and general construction of the implant itself. Once you leave the operating table with a new hip, half the job has been completed. The other half is up to you.

LIFESTYLE CHANGES

"Lifestyle changes" is a loaded term that tends to evoke about as much enthusiasm as the words "Christmas shopping." Some people love roaming the department stores, but many of us shudder at the thought of draining our wallets to buy overpriced goods that will be discarded by our offspring within a few months. Likewise, most people who have reached middle age have their routines pretty well established. If they smoked, drank, worked too hard, played too long, and enjoyed sedentary lives before the surgery, it is unlikely that they will wildly embrace the thought of changing their diet and lifestyle following a THR.

CIGARETTES

There are hundreds of good reasons to stop smoking but how can smoking affect your hip? Smoking interferes with the circulation of blood and in order to keep your hip and other joints and muscles healthy, you want an optimum amount of blood flowing to the femoral head. Also, nonsmokers have stronger bones. The web site *Why Quit Smoking* states that, "Following the fracture of any bone within the human body, the average length of time for a non-smoker to form 1 cm of new bone is 69.6 days as compared with 89.4 days for smokers." Smokers have a higher incidence of colds, bronchitis, and infections, which is something that you will definitely want to avoid after your hip replacement.

I was the last one in my family to quit smoking at the ripe age of 46. I had already cut down to four cigarettes a day for many years, but I looked forward to every one with an almost religious zeal. I had specific time slots for each of my daily smokes and created elaborate rituals around them. I inhaled. I exhaled. I loved those cigarettes and relinquished them with great reluctance. I even owned a baseball cap that said, "I gave up smoking, drinking and sex and it was the worst three hours of my life!" Thus, I can certainly sympathize with anyone who dreads the thought of parting with their nicotine. The good news is that the craving for cigarettes does pass. I can honestly say that I never think about smoking now except in a disparaging way.

FOOD

Another variable that is likely to affect your new hip is your weight. It stands to reason that being overweight will place a strain on your joint. Imagine if I gave you a suitcase filled with forty pounds of bricks and asked you to carry it around all day. That's how your new hip feels when it is forced to carry your extra weight. There is also a greater likelihood of dislocating the prosthesis if a person is overweight. Giving up food may be even more difficult than letting go of cigarettes. If you're tired of gaining and losing weight with Slim Fast, the Zone diet, South Beach or the Protein Power Plan, try to cut back your food gradually. Even a 10 to 15 pound reduction in weight will make a difference in the amount of pressure that is being applied to your joint.

On the other hand, you don't want to get too thin, especially if you're female. After menopause, women lose calcium from their bones and are more prone to osteoporosis, a softening of the bones, which can lead to hip fractures. Women who have a little more meat on their bones are less likely to get osteoporosis. So, have that piece of pie! Just have a small slice.

Basically, I follow a modified version of the Atkins diet to keep my blood sugar stable. I often feel deprived of carbohydrates and sweets and I do cheat sometimes. But I have been much more faithful to my diet since I had my hip replaced because I have felt less depressed, and have not had the need to reach out to food to comfort me. In fact, I can only count three occasions where I broke my diet in a big way since my hip surgery one year ago, including the holidays when I had to indulge in a small piece of my mother's Icelandic Christmas cake. Although I don't diet to stay slim, following the Atkins plan keeps me at an ideal weight, which is good for my new hip. And there are some satisfying foods to eat on the program like peanuts, bacon, steak and cheese.

EXERCISE AND ACTIVITY

Your new hip is much like a new car. Unlike a new house, whose value may appreciate over the years, your new hip will depreciate. Like a car, your prosthesis may be perfect when you receive it or it may be mediocre. In some unfortunate instances, your implant may be "a lemon." Regardless of the shape of your implant when it was first inserted, it will wear out over time. Therefore, use will affect the lifespan of your hip. If you overuse it or abuse it, it will reward you by deteriorating faster. On the other hand, just like a car, idleness and inactivity are bad for your implant. How much exercise and activity do you need for your new hip? Moderation is the key.

Exercise is strongly recommended postoperatively because the prosthesis works better if it is well supported by strong muscles. Certain sports and activities are much better for your hip than others. It is widely agreed that walking and swimming are excellent for the new hip. Golfing is considered to be safe as long as the golfer does not rotate or twist the hips excessively. Working out on a stationary bicycle is fine; just make sure that you adjust the seat of the bicycle high enough so that your knees are not pedaling higher than your hips. Conversely, there is a consensus in the medical community that jogging, climbing, and jarring the hip are potentially dangerous. However, there are different schools of thought about other forms of exercise.

Generally, skiing, basketball, baseball, hockey, racquetball, volleyball, soccer, and football are considered taboo. Walking on a treadmill and playing singles tennis are also discouraged, although many people do return to tennis by playing double sets, which require less running. Other people like Ronald Allen, law professor and co-author of *Arthritis of the Hip & Knee*, do resume singles tennis. Allen was a sport and could not bear to part with his favorite activity. After his total hip replacement, Allen's regular physiotherapy regimen did not provide him with enough muscular strength and flexibility for him to feel comfortable climbing stairs and playing tennis again. Consequently, he undertook a more sophisticated physiotherapy program. Allen was not content to return to functioning. He wanted to return to fitness, which required more time and effort on his part. And he was willing to take the risk that his hip may dislocate because he wanted to play tennis so badly. In fact, Allen did injure his new hip but not by playing tennis. He fell on the ice when he was skating with his sons, and broke the top of his femur. His hip was never the same again.

Roller skating, downhill skiing, outdoor bicycling, horseback riding, and hiking are in the same category with ice skating. Many people who have hip replacements return to these activities, especially cycling, but they are advised to use caution when doing so. Comedian Denis Leary once said that he had no intention of quitting cigarettes. "People always say that smoking takes ten years off your life," Leary quipped. "Well, it's the ten worst years, isn't it folks? It's the ones at the end! It's the wheelchair, adult diaper years. You can have those years, all right? We don't want them!" Leary added. Some people feel that way about sports. They would rather lead full and active lives now in their fifties or sixties, rather than worry about what may happen if they need several hip revisions that will render them disabled 20 years from now. They also hope that by the time they need their second or third revision, modern medicine will have advanced significantly and may even have developed a permanent hip replacement that will last a lifetime.

Personally, I'm not much of a risk taker when it comes to my health. Luckily, I'm not much of a jock either. In Sartre's play *No Exit*, hell on earth is portrayed as three people who don't like each other being stuck in the same room together for eternity. My version of *No Exit* is to be trapped in a spinning class with Richard Simmons and 20 other sweaty bodies, all mouthing the words, "Nautilus." I don't like organized aerobic activities. However, I do enjoy swimming and bicycling, and I absolutely love ice skating. I learned to skate when I was five years old. Aside from walking, it is one of my favorite sports. When I asked my surgeon if I could skate again, he paused and said, "You can skate with caution but if you fall, it is likely that you will break your hip." That said it all for me! I will benefit by Ronald Allen's unfortunate experience. I will not take that chance. Several hours or years of exhilaration on the ice rink would never be worth it to me if I needed to have revision surgery five years from now. You may choose differently.

POSITIONS

Some doctors, like Richard Villar, advise adhering to the 90 degree precaution for an indefinite period of time because they think that is safer for your hip. Most surgeons only recommend maintaining a 90 degree angle for the first six to ten weeks postoperatively. Usually, around the time that the precautions are discontinued, the hip patient can return to driving a car. Thereafter, patients are warned against sitting in chairs that are too low or sitting cross-legged, although some people like Thelma Lubkin are willing to take the risk of assuming that position. Physicians are not always in agreement about whether or not it is safe to cross one's legs following a hip replacement. Some doctors say that it is best not to cross your legs at all. Some suggest not crossing your legs repeatedly. Others, like my own surgeon, state that it is all right to cross the good leg over the bad leg, but not vice versa, and that it is permissible to cross one's legs at the ankle. Check with your own doctor about safe positions and remember your mother's sage advice — when in doubt, don't!

SEX

Like Villar, Irwin Silber advocates not flexing the hip beyond 90 degrees for life. At the same time, he says that you can resume sexual activities about six weeks after the surgery. "What's stopping you?" Silber asks. "Just don't be too acrobatic." This seems a bit contradictory to me. I'm hard-pressed to envision how someone can have intercourse while abiding by the precautions, although Silber did include several interesting illustrations of "safe sex" positions for the post-op patient. Frankly, two months after hip surgery, the thought of lovemaking appealed to me about as much as the thought of drinking a can of Drano. Moreover, I found that when I asked my occupational therapist and my physiotherapist when I could resume sexual activities, I received different answers based on the specificity of my questions.

In the hospital, I asked my occupational therapist (OT) in the short-term rehab unit when it would be safe to have sex again. She said that usually, people could couple about eight weeks after surgery. The position that she suggested involved the patient on his or her back, regardless of their gender. Since I had no interest in sex at that point, I did not make further inquiries until I was in outpatient physiotherapy at the hospital. Then I asked my physio the same question and she seemed puzzled. She said that the question didn't come up that often, possibly because most of her hip replacement patients were older, but she would check with the OT. The physio received an e-mail from the OT, which said pretty much the same thing that the OT had told me in the hospital. But this time, it occurred to me to ask the physio if it was all right if I wrapped my legs around the back of my partner's legs during sex and she shouted, "No! You could dislocate in that position." Her alarming reaction made me feel as though I should forget about sex with human beings altogether and stick with an inflatable doll. I received completely different answers from the professionals based on the questions that I had asked. This taught me that I needed to be concrete and specific when I queried people if I wanted to truly protect my new hip.

Silber's safe sex positions seemed more appropriate for men than for women but some could be used for either gender. His pictures included one with a male patient on top and his partner on the bottom in the standard missionary position. Another drawing had a male patient lying on his side with his operated leg on top of his partner's leg. This looked risky to me but the third illustration looked manageable. That picture showed a patient standing up and approaching his female partner from behind with her bending slightly forward. Two photos of unsafe positions included a man sitting on a chair with a female partner on top of him, and a man lying on his back with his knees flexed and a female partner on top of him. Linda May-Bowser also has a number of helpful illustrations and guidelines for safe sex postoperatively on her *Totally Hip* web site, which is located at http://members.tripod.com/totallyhip1/educate/sexthr.htm.

CALCIUM

If you are female, you have probably heard news broadcasts and read numerous articles about the importance of adding calcium to your diet. Calcium and vitamin D are essential minerals for building and maintaining strong bones for both men and women. Calcium can be found in most dairy products including milk, cheese, and yogurt as well as in enriched orange juice and green leafy vegetables like broccoli or kale. Tofu is a good source of calcium but soy milk is not unless it has been enriched. The best sources of vitamin D come from fish and fish oils but beware of consuming too much canned tuna, fresh tuna, shark or swordfish due to the possibility of mercury poisoning. Recent news bulletins also indicate that there are contaminants in farmed salmon. Sometimes women remove dairy products from their diet because these foods are fattening. Other times, people avoid dairy because they are allergic to it and soy because they don't like it. If you can't get enough calcium or vitamin D in your food, consider taking a supplement.

AVOIDING INFECTION

There is a small chance that your implant can become infected years after the surgery. You will want to take special precautions to avoid infections in general by taking good care of yourself. The American Dental Association and the American Academy of Orthopaedic Surgeons agree that if you have an infection anywhere in your body, such as your urinary tract, stomach, lungs, skin or mouth, you should contact your doctor immediately to see if you need antibiotics. Because bacteria can travel from any part of the body to your prosthesis, surgeons recommend that you take prophylactic antibiotics before dental visits and any other minor surgery. This includes having your teeth cleaned since the procedure is likely to make your gums bleed and expel bacteria into the bloodstream. The Dental Association and Academy of Orthopaedic Surgeons states, "Antibiotic prophylaxis is not indicated for dental patients with pins, plates and screws, nor is it routinely indicated for most dental patients with total joint replacements. However, it is advisable to consider premedication in a small number of patients who may be at potential increased risk of hematogenous total joint infection." Those who are at increased risk include people with compromised immune systems, insulin-dependent diabetics, people who have had previous infections in their hip implants, hemophiliacs, those who are malnourished, and *anyone who has had a total joint replacement within the last two years*. After two years, the prophylactic antibiotics may be discontinued.

10

The Future of Hip Replacements

The future of total hip replacements depends on a number of factors including the prevention and treatment of arthritis, changes in the design and materials used in THR implants, and the results of innovative research on stem cells and cartilage transplantation. The extent of waiting lists, delays in receiving insurance approval for the operation, and the availability of orthopedists will also influence joint replacement surgery in years to come.

ARTHRITIS PREVENTION

Some forms of arthritis are preventable like the post-traumatic osteoarthritis that is caused by an injury. Children can be taught the importance of using caution and good judgment in contact sports in order to reduce the risk of spraining a ligament or fracturing a joint, which could lead to arthritis later on in life. Many sports injuries can be avoided by simply ensuring that a child is wearing equipment that fits properly, including helmets and protective eye gear. Playing surfaces should be examined for potholes and basketball courts should not be made out of cement. In hockey, larger playing fields reduce the risk of injury, as does the practice of prohibiting body checking for younger children. Drinking plenty of fluids also helps to keep children hydrated.

Encouraging kids to stretch or warm up before a game may reduce sprains and stress fractures. Reinjury is common when children return to playing sports without allowing sufficient time for a strain or sprain to heal. Kids are frequently injured by overusing muscles. Spondylolysis, a form of arthritis, often results from trauma or repetitive use. Spondylolysis is commonly seen in football, weight lifting, gymnastics, and diving and is more common in girls than boys.

The same rules of caution in sports that apply to children are relevant to adults. The American Academy of Orthopaedic Surgeons claims that more women than men experience stress fractures. Women are susceptible to what is called the "female athlete triad;" eating disorders, loss of menstrual cycle, and osteoporosis, a decrease in bone density, which predisposes women to stress fractures.

Having a greater awareness of wet slippery surfaces can decrease the number of falls, which may lead to a broken hip. Ordinary activities such as getting out of a swimming pool or bathtub and walking on snow or black ice can be hazardous, especially to older people. The mortality rate following a hip fracture in an older person is high. Researchers at the University of Maryland have found that men have a higher risk of death following a hip fracture than do women. Within one year of breaking their hips, 31 percent of men and 15 percent of women in this study died. Mortality rates after two years were 42 percent in men and 23 percent in women. Most fractures occur in women; men account for only 25 to 30 percent of all hip fractures.

Wearing seat belts and employing sobriety checkpoints can reduce the number of cases of osteoarthritis that are related to car accidents. According to the Center for Disease Control, alcohol-related crashes and fatalities were reduced from 18 percent to 24 percent with the introduction of sobriety checkpoints. Checkpoints allow police officers to stop vehicles in a specific sequence, such as every other vehicle or every third, fourth, or fifth vehicle. My injury and subsequent need for a joint replacement could also have been avoided if the drunk driver who hit me had been mandated to alcohol treatment after his first or second driving offense.

ARTHRITIS TREATMENT

Some forms of arthritis are genetic. In the future, researchers may discover the different genetic factors that contribute to both osteoarthritis and rheumatoid arthritis. This may lead to drugs or procedures that will target the specific disease process and delay or reduce inflammation and deterioration of the hip joint.

We have seen a new class of drugs emerge for treating arthritis within the last decade. Celebrex and Vioxx are more potent than

107

aspirin, Advil and Tylenol, but may still cause gastric upset. We also have medications for osteoporosis that build bones like Didrocal, Actonel and Fosamax. Perhaps, future treatment of arthritis will involve using drugs (with minimal side effects) that can regenerate cartilage or build back lost bone around the hip joint.

Arthritis may be detected at an earlier stage by injecting a chemical into the joint. This will improve the image obtained through magnetic resonance imaging (MRI) and will enable radiologists to detect damage to the joint even before the cartilage begins to deteriorate. Early detection and treatment of an arthritic hip may prevent the need for joint replacement entirely.

NEW SURGICAL ADVANCES

New surgical techniques are on the horizon, including the development of procedures that are less invasive than a THR. Allen, Brander, and Stulberg state that robots have already been employed to perform hip replacements in conjunction with a surgeon. They believe that computer-assisted technology may improve the accuracy with which implants are inserted. However, given the potential for computer hardware and software failure, I would prefer to have a person operating on me rather than a machine. If NASA's space shuttles can explode and their Mars Spirit rover can develop signal failures 150 million miles away from home, there is always the possibility that a robot could make a serious error conducting hip surgery, even if it operated along with a team.

Other inventions seem more promising to me. A group in Israel recently performed a minimally invasive total hip replacement. Approximately 500 joint replacements are performed each year at the Center for Joint Replacement at Hadassah Hospital at Mount Scopus. The minimal invasion method began to be used by Hadassah's orthopedists about two years ago. So far, 50 operations have been performed but until recently, the process severed the muscles around the joint.

In 2003, surgeons at Hadassah conducted a THR without severing the muscles around the hip joint. "During this experimental surgery, two incisions of approximately 6 centimeters (2.4 inches) were made, instead of 20 centimeter (8 inches) incisions. The patient, who underwent this surgery, was able to get down from his bed about 12 hours after the operation and began to walk freely with very minimal pain," the Hadassah Medical Organization declares. This surgery is not appropriate for every patient, but when it is suitable, an individual can return to normal functioning quickly. Time spent in the hospital is also significantly reduced.

THE IMPLANTS

As the population ages and more hip replacements are performed, it will be critical to continue improving the strength and durability of the implants. Younger and more active patients will require implants that are made of stronger materials. Currently, the typical prosthesis is made of a metal head with a plastic or polyethylene cup. Several other designs are being investigated including an implant with a metal head and a metal cup. This is what Edward Marshall, one of my interviewees, received. Michael Bentley, who had his hip resurfaced, was also given a prosthesis composed entirely of metal parts.

Metal-on-metal is less likely to wear out over time than metal on plastic, but such implants are costly and there is concern that metal is a toxin. The Joint Replacement Center at Florida Hospital claims that metal-on-metal total hip replacements result in higher levels of colbalt and chromium in the blood and urine. Like other heavy metals, such as lead, this may result in a greater risk of developing cancer. However, some forms of metal-on-metal implants have been used for over three decades, and there has not been any indication that these patients are at an increased risk for cancer.

The Joint Replacement Center provides detailed information regarding the rate at which different prosthetic components deteriorate: "The average linear wear rate of a metal head on a plastic liner is 0.1 — 0.2 millimeter per year. The average linear wear rate of a metal head on a metal liner is approximately 0.005 millimeter per year. The average linear wear rate of a ceramic head on a ceramic liner is approximately 0.001 millimeter per year. The average linear wear rate of a metal head on a highly crosslinked polyethylene liner is approximately 0.005 — 0.01 millimeter per year. When the linear wear reaches approximately 1.5 — 2.0 millimeters, we typically begin to see problems with the hip replacement. Therefore, it is small wonder that we begin to see significant problems with total hip replacements in the 10 to 20 year range (10 years times 0.15 millimeter per year equals 1.5 millimeter of wear.)"

The lifespan of a traditional hip replacement with a metal head in a plastic socket is approximately 10 to 15 years. Often, the metal head does not have to be replaced after this time, but the plastic socket does. An implant made with crosslinked polyethylene may last 20 to 25 years, according to the GAMC, the Glendale Adventist Medical Center in Arizona. The longest lasting implants are made of ceramic. It is estimated that the ceramic hip may last 50 to 60 years, which is equivalent to lasting a lifetime for most joint recipients. These are only estimates because the ceramic hip is so new that there are no long-term studies on its actual longevity.

THE CERAMIC HIP

Simply by changing from a metal to a ceramic head, wear can be reduced by 50 percent or more. Golf pro Jack Nicklaus chose to have a ceramic hip, even before the implant received FDA approval in February of 2003. "My doctor, Ben Bierbaum, told me all about the new design and ceramic-on-ceramic materials they were using in the hip," Nicklaus says. "He told me if I got the metal and plastic hip that's commonly used, I would be back in four or five years because of my activity level." Nicklaus claims that the decision to go with a ceramic rather than a metal and plastic hip was easy to make, since the latter would probably have involved more surgery in five years.

Ceramic is stronger than any other material except diamond, which is why it can last almost indefinitely. It is also possible to create a larger femoral head using a ceramic replacement. With a metal and plastic design, femoral heads usually range about 28 millimeters in size, whereas a ceramic ball may be as large as 32 to 36 millimeters. This enables the ball to fit more securely in the socket, which leads some surgeons to believe that the larger head will reduce the risk of dislocation.

As exciting as it sounds, the new ceramic hip has its disadvantages. First, it is almost twice as expensive as a traditional hip replacement. Since conventional implants work well for most people over the age of 65, Medicare, Medicaid, insurance companies and national health care systems may prefer to employ the cheaper model. Secondly, ceramic implants had a high rate of failure in their early days. The use of ceramics in THRs dates back over 30 years in Europe. In 1970, Boutin implanted the first ceramic-on-ceramic cemented hip replacement in France. Some of the ceramic hips fractured early on. Later failures were the result of loosening due to osteolysis and design flaws that were not related to the ceramic bearing. Thirdly, Ronald Grelsamer, M.D., orthopedic surgeon at the NYU Hospital for Joint Diseases, and author of *What Your Doctor May Not Tell You about Hip and Knee Replacement Surgery*, states that the ceramic implant's lack of a protective lip around the back of the prosthetic cup may result in a greater chance of dislocation. In many ways, they are "fragile," Grelsamer says, and are reserved for patients who are "young, heavy and active."

However, new materials have significantly decreased the risk that a ceramic hip may become brittle and crack. A recent study on 60 patients at the Marshfield Clinic Research Foundation in Wisconsin demonstrated that the ceramic hip worked very well. "A type of ceramic called alumina is used specifically for prosthetic hips," says Dr. Cameron of the Foundation. It does not react adversely with the body. It has generally been found to be quite successful, and has very few problems."

51-year-old Tom D'Urso of St. George, Vermont is a marathon runner. Like Nicklaus, D'Urso knew that a traditional replacement would destroy his life as an athlete; he now runs 70 miles per week with his ceramic implant and has not encountered any problems with his new hip so far. "Even though the wear is less, no orthopedic surgeon is going to recommend to go out and do what Tom does," his physician, Dr. Stephen Murphy of Boston cautions. "Tom's activity level is higher than anyone I know, artificial hip or not. We don't know if his hip will last five, 10, 20 years or if he'll have to have it redone earlier. He's an amazing person, but I can't tell him it's a safe thing to do."

CROSSLINKING

The use of a highly crosslinked polyethylene liner, like my own, will significantly increase the durability of the hip replacement prosthesis. According to Zimmer, the manufacturer, "A simplified analogy of conventional polyethylene versus highly crosslinked polyethylene, is a wicker basket that has all the strands going in one direction (conventional polyethylene) versus a wicker basket that has strands going in two directions (highly crosslinked polyethylene.)" This material has been used now for more than five years and studies show that it is highly wear-resistant. Active Joints.com claims that the crosslinked polyethylene wears at a rate of about 1/10th or less the rate of the standard polyethylene, which significantly increases the lifespan of the implant.

POROUS COATINGS

A new porous coating for hip implants has been developed at Oxford University. Its goal is to encourage bone growth and it was designed for younger, more active patients. "Implants are mainly successful in patients aged 55 or older," said Peter Wilshaw from the Department of Materials at the University of Oxford, and one of the inventors of the new coating. "The problem comes when you are faced with younger patients." Conventional cementless replacements tend to use a compound called hydroxyapatite, which can break down in the body. This may lead to bone loss and ultimately to implant failure. Wilshaw and his colleague, Eva Palsgard, from the Centre for Surface Biotechnology at the University of Uppsala, Sweden, have invented a porous inorganic coating. This aluminum coating enables the bone to grow into the implant and bond to it. The more securely the implant is fixed to the bone, the longer it will last. Wilshaw believes that an implant coated with his porous material could last up to 30 years. Implants with the aluminum coating are not available yet commercially but could appear within the next five years.

STEM CELLS

A study published in the December 2003 issue of *The Journal of Dental Research* indicates that researchers at the University of Illinois at Chicago have turned adult stem cells into bone and cartilage. This procedure has only been tested in animals so far, but it has resulted in the formation of a ball structure similar to that found in the human jaw. "This represents the first time a human-shaped joint, with both cartilage and a bone-like tissue, was grown from a single population of adult stem cells," says Jeremy Mao, director of the Tissue Engineering laboratory in the UIC College of Dentistry, and Associate Professor of bioengineering and orthodontics. Someday, the tissue-engineering procedure could be used to regenerate the ball portion of joints in the jaw, knee, and hip that have been damaged by injury or arthritis.

Likewise, BST-CarGel by Biosyntech of Laval, Quebec has the potential to generate cartilage. CarGel, a polysaccharide or complex carbohydrate, is mixed with a patient's blood. Surgeons then make a tiny incision in the bone and fill it with CarGel. The mixture acts as a catalyst so that the stem cells of the bone marrow begin to regenerate articular cartilage. CarGel has not yet received official approval for human trials; however, three male patients have already been treated with the substance under Health Canada's Special Access Program for medical devices. All of the men had cartilage inserted into their knees in order to prevent the need for a total knee replacement. Businessman and hockey star, Serge Savard, is one of the three patients who are currently living "pain-free, with brand-new cartilage," Biosyntech declares. By the end of 2004, studies will have been conducted on a hundred patients for the Canadian and American markets.

Dr. Rita Kandel at Mount Sinai Hospital in Toronto has developed a procedure that regenerates cartilage. The new cartilage was implanted into arthritic joints to replace damaged cartilage. "Over the next few years, this kind of treatment could greatly improve the long-term mobility of many people with osteoarthritis," notes her colleague, Dr. Ken Pritzker, chief of pathology at Mount Sinai Hospital. To date, the cartilage regeneration has only been tested on animals.

HIP SURGERY CENTERS

As time goes on, we may see the creation of more hip surgery centers, where the only operations performed are total hip replacements. As younger people have primary hip replacements, we will see an increase in the number of hip revision specialists. Certain orthopedists will specialize in revisions and implant manufacturers will focus their research on improving the lifespan of a second or third hip implant. The specific biological, mechanical, and rehabilitation variables that affect the outcome of revision surgery will also be explored in more depth.

The long-term results of hip resurfacing will be seen and this less invasive procedure, which results in fewer restrictions postoperatively, may become available to larger numbers of people.

THE GRAYING OF THE POPULATION

As the population ages and expands, the demand for orthopedic care will increase. The Canadian Orthopaedic Foundation states that in the future, there will be more arthritis, osteoporosis, falls and fractures. This will lead to a greater need for orthopedic surgery, particularly hip and knee replacements. Studies conducted by the Mayo Clinic and the University of Edmonton in Alberta suggest that even people in their eighties and nineties may benefit by a total hip replacement. Excellent results were achieved with both primary and revision arthroplasties performed on these older people, although the Mayo Clinic group had certain preexisting conditions, such as cardiac problems or anemia, which made the surgery more difficult.

Dr. James O'Brien, M.D. of the Department of Family and Community Medicine at the University of Louisville Health Sciences Center, notes that the study "provides a glimpse into the future and highlights the challenge that physicians, orthopedists in particular, are likely to confront." He says that the most rapidly growing segment of the United States population is the group 85 years and older. "But perhaps even more dramatic is the increase in centenarians (those age 100 and older) with a predicted doubling each decade in the future," Dr. O'Brien exclaims. "Thus, treatment of this age group will become much more commonplace."

HMOs

Some theorists have predicted the demise of the HMO but that seems unlikely given its domination of the health care market. In the movie *John Q.*, a desperate man holds a physician and an entire emergency room hostage when his HMO refuses to pay for life saving surgery on his son. Few people would take such drastic action, but many consumers and doctors can relate to John's despair and frustration with the way that HMOs cut costs, often at the expense of the patient's health. "The science of medicine may have made dazzling advances, but the delivery of medicine continues to be a major disappointment. You can buy a personal computer over the Internet, but you still have to take a half-day off from work to see your doctor," says Ronald Henkoff of Fortune magazine.

Henkoff recommends the book *Market-Driven Health Care: Who Wins, Who Loses in the Transformation of America's Largest Service Industry* by Regina Herzlinger. A Harvard business school professor, Herzlinger believes the inconvenient and often inequitable health care system can be improved. In her book, Herzlinger discusses the possibility of establishing specialized clinics that are reasonably priced and efficient: what Henkoff refers to as the "health care equivalents of Wal-Mart." The clinics would provide all of the specialists that patients need situated under one roof. Located in shopping malls, clinics would be open days, nights, and weekends. A patient with chronic eczema could be treated at a skin-care center staffed with doctors, nurses, pharmacists, psychologists, and cosmeticians.

In 2002, HMOs dropped almost 500,000 American seniors. Hundreds of thousands of HMOs pulled out of Medicare. In the future, seniors may have to pay a monthly premium, which they may not have had to do before, according to Julie Rovner, a reporter who covers health policy for *National Journal's Congress Daily*. "You'll probably have to pay more for drugs if there is a drug benefit and more to see doctors, more in the way of co-payments. If you live in areas where Medicare doesn't pay so well, you may not have any choice of health plans. You may have to go back to the traditional Medicare program and if you can, get private supplemental Medigap insurance."

WAITING FOR GODOT

As the demand for orthopedic care in Canada increases, the number of orthopedic surgeons has declined. Canada has approximately 900 orthopedic surgeons today. "It's estimated that at least 150 new orthopedic specialists are needed to meet current requirements — let alone future demands," the Canadian Orthopaedic Foundation declares. There are sixteen training programs in Canada for orthopedic specialists, and approximately the same number of orthopedic residents is graduating from these programs today as did in the 1970s. In the last two years or so, the number of doctors applying to orthopedics has decreased. This will lead to serious problems down the road by increasing the length of time that a person in need of hip surgery will have to wait.

Hospital overcrowding in Canada presents additional problems for patients. For example, in Ottawa, hospital emergency rooms are so overtaxed that ambulances are frequently turned away and redirected to other hospitals. This means that if I were to suddenly fall and break my new hip, I may not be able to see my own surgeon. It is entirely possible that I could call an ambulance and ask to be taken to my hospital, only to be told that it was not receiving patients. Consequently, I would have to go to another hospital and be seen by a total stranger.

The Canadian Orthopaedic Association and the Arthritis Society claim that more than twice as many Canadians have osteoarthritis as have heart disease, and that more than six times as many have arthritis as have cancer. The two groups have proposed a national strategy to deal with the problem of waiting lists. The plan calls for "national standards for orthopedic waiting times, improved access to care, especially for people in rural and underserviced areas, and recruiting and retaining more orthopedic surgeons." Dr. Michael Stanger, president of the British Columbia Orthopaedic Association, says that studies obtained by his group indicate that "access to care is in serious jeopardy. The problem is reaching crisis proportions."

One would think that unreasonably long waiting lists would influence Canadians to vote for the establishment of a private health care system, which would run parallel to the existing national system. But Canadians value their social medicine too much to approve the mass use of private facilities. This is unfortunate because if people who could afford to pay for their own medical care left the public domain, it would significantly decrease the waiting time for those who cannot afford to pay. However, if a two-tiered system is ever seriously considered in Canada — and I personally doubt that it will be — provisions must be made to ensure that patients who remain in the public realm receive a high quality of care and that all doctors continue to take public patients.

Despite the antipathy that Canadians have towards the concept of privatizing medicine, private clinics are already operating in Ontario, British Columbia, Alberta and Quebec, where the waiting time for a consultation with an orthopedic surgeon may be as short as one week. The average wait within the traditional system is 13.3 weeks. Certainly, anyone with connections in Canada can bypass the queue or go to the U.S. for treatment, thus, waiting lists have less impact on the wealthy.

RESEARCH

Further research is necessary to determine the long-term safety of total joint implants. Do the materials used in the prosthesis, such as metal and plastic, cause adverse systemic side effects as they accumulate? Do they cause cancer or genetic abnormalities in the children of patients who have had joint replacements? Thus far, we have not seen any systemic effects but as the length of time that people have implants increases, studies will look for long-term side effects, particularly when implants are done in young people.

The materials and the manufacturing process currently used for THR implants have been vastly improved in terms of their design and finish. But aside from the ceramic hip, most implants continue to wear out too quickly. More research is needed in order to analyze the ability of current implants to grow into the bone and provide a stable long-term fixation. New instruments and more experience will lead to higher amounts of bone ingrowth in uncemented implants. Different types of bone cement will improve the bonding between the cement and the bone. Improvement in the technique of applying bone cement will also be the focus of future studies. Ongoing research will enhance our understanding of the wear process that can prolong the life of the implant.

The National Institute of Health in the United States has recommended a national study of hip implants that have been retrieved from cadavers. This would provide significant information about why implants fail. The NIH also advocates clinical trials to assess the efficacy of implant designs and surgical approaches, including the effect of coatings that encourage bone growth for fixation and the specific mechanisms associated with osteolysis. And the Institute suggests an improvement of existing patient education, preoperatively and postoperatively.

Factors like age, sex, weight, activity level, and coexisting medical conditions need to be studied in relation to their effect on hip surgery. Ethnicity, income level, and geographic location should also be examined since there is some evidence that certain groups may not have equal access to total hip surgery, based on their race, gender or location.

Finally, the National Institute of Health recommends the establishment of both regional and national registries in the United States, like the Canadian Joint Replacement Registry, which began in the summer of 2000. The Board of Directors of the American Academy of Orthopaedic Surgeons approved a study of the feasibility of establishing a national total joint registry at a meeting held in 2001; a pilot project to collect registry data was also sanctioned. The Swedish National Hip Arthroplasty Register, started more than 20 years ago, describes the patient characteristics and reasons for implant failure of total hip replacements performed in Sweden. A national registry in the U.S. would collect data on all THR and revision procedures. "The goals of this registry should be to better define the natural history and epidemiology of THR in the U.S. population as a whole, and to identify risk factors for poor outcomes that relate to the implant, procedure, and patient characteristics," the NIH declares.

THE BLOOD SUPPLY

The United States is currently experiencing a shortage of blood. The American Association of Blood Banks, America's Blood Centers and the American Red Cross are requesting donations to increase dangerously low supplies. Ordinarily, blood supplies drop in the winter; holidays, bad weather and illness often prevent individuals from donating during this time and more people are injured in traffic accidents and require transfusions. Inventories have fallen well below safe and sufficient levels. Certain blood types are almost depleted and in some areas of the country, elective surgeries have been postponed or cancelled. Secretary of Health and Human Services, Tommy G. Thompson, said in January of 2004, "The nation is facing critical shortages in communities across the country. If blood supplies do not immediately increase, patients, accident victims and those whose lives depend on regular transfusions, are at risk for not getting the blood they need. Every eligible individual should give blood, if not for themselves, for their friends, their loved ones or their neighbors."

Canada's blood supply is adequate but could still use bolstering. In a 2001 article published by Joanne Stassen, Michelle van Vliet of Canadian Blood Services in Ottawa claimed that "75 percent of Canadians are willing to give blood, and 50 percent are eligible, yet only three percent do so." According to Derek Mellon, Media Relations Manager of the Canadian Blood Services, that number rose to 3.7 percent by 2004, thanks to the institution of an appointment system, which allowed donors to book appointments to give blood. An aggressive marketing campaign to educate the public about the problem was also established, and the formation of a national call center helped to recruit more donors. Mellon informed me that Canadian Blood Services is presently meeting hospital demands, but that doing so "is a struggle," and that they would love to enlarge the percentage of donors to 5 percent.

Donations dropped after October of 2001 when the safety of the blood supply was in question. Although there is no definitive proof that mad cow disease can be transmitted through blood, such a fear has led to new restrictions on donors; they may not be eligible to give blood if they have spent a cumulative total of three months or more in the United Kingdom or France since 1980, or if they have spent a cumulative total of five years or more in Western Europe outside the U.K. or France since 1980. Moreover, people are not eligible to donate blood or plasma if they have had a blood transfusion in the U.K. since 1980.

While donors have declined, the need for blood has grown, partly because traditional volunteers have become too old to donate. Also, as the population ages, people are requiring more surgery. The Canadian Blood Services states that there has been a "45 percent increase in total knee replacements and an almost 20 percent increase in total hip replacements between 1995 and 2000."

119

THE AGE OF INFORMATION

The Internet has dramatically changed our ability to obtain information. Patients are just one mouse click away from learning more about their arthritis. A quick search on Yahoo! listed 943,000 web sites related to hip replacement in June of 2004, with the numbers growing monthly. Government agencies, such as the National Institute of Health are also online. Medical databases like Medline or PubMed are readily available and both the American Academy of Orthopaedic Surgeons and the Canadian Orthopaedic Foundation provide a wealth of information on total hip replacements. Prospective surgical candidates can join chat lines and discussion groups in order to talk to other people who have had THRs. People can learn from one another, gain emotional support, or read published medical articles from peer reviewed journals without ever having to leave their room. Recently, two cannibals met each other on an Internet newsgroup and created quite an international controversy. If such an obscure couple could find each other online, surely the millions of people who have had total hip replacements should be able to easily connect with one another!

CONCLUSIONS

Aside from the lengthy waiting lists plaguing patients in countries with socialized medicine, and the continued frustration that many Americans experience with their HMOs and Medicare, the future of total hip replacements looks very promising. New coatings and bearing surfaces for implants will increase the longevity of hip replacements. If they prove to be safe and reliable, both metal-on-metal and ceramic hips have the potential to last a lifetime. We may be able to dispense with surgery entirely if tissue-engineering procedures and products like CarGel are durable and effective. But until these sophisticated advances materialize, take good care of your present hip and enjoy your newfound mobility if you have just received a hip replacement.

BIBLIOGRAPHY

About.com Arthritis. "Age and Joint Replacement Studied." 15 December, 2003. <http://arthritis.about.com/gi/dynamic/offsite. htm?site=http%3A%2F%2Fwww.arthritissupport.com%2Flibrar y%2Fshowarticle.cfm%3FID%3D238>

_____. "Over 90% Highly Satisfied with Joint Replacement Surgery." 15 December, 2003. <http://arthritis.about.com/gi/ dynamic/offsite.htm?site=http%3A%2F%2F0www.intelihealth. com%2FIH%2FihtIH%2FEMIHC000%2F333%2F8896%2F311 282.html>

_____. "Too Young for Joint Replacement." 15 December, 2003. <http://arthritis.about.com/cs/jtreplace/a/youngjtreplace.htm>

Active Joints.com. "Hip Joint Treatments for Active Patients: Surgical Options." 22 December, 2003. <http://www.activejoints.com/ hipreplacement.html>

Aetna InteliHealth. "Hip Replacement." 1 January, 2004. <http:// www.intelihealth.com/IH/ihtIH/WSIHW000/9071/9218/200783. html?d=DmtContent>

Allen, Ronald J., Brander, Dr. Victoria Anne, and Stulberg, Dr. S. David. *Arthritis of the Hip & Knee: The Active Person's Guide to Taking Charge.* Atlanta: Peachtree Publishers, 1998.

American Academy of Orthopaedic Surgeons. "Arthroplasty and Total Joint Replacement Procedures." 18 November, 2003. <http://www.aaos.org/wordhtml/research/stats/stats_3.htm>

_____. "Deep Vein Thrombosis." 18 November, 2003. <http://ortho info.aaos.org/fact/thr_report.cfm?Thread_ID=264&topcategory =Hip>

_____. "Hip Dislocation." 18 November, 2003. <http://orthoinfo. aaos.org/fact /thr_report.cfm?Thread_ID=175&topcategory=Hip>

_____. "Hip Implants." 18 November, 2003. <http://orthoinfo.aaos. org/fact/thr_report.cfm?Thread_ID=271&topcategory=Hip>

_____. "Improving Musculoskeletal Care in America: Osteoarthritis of the Hip." (IMCA) Information Series. 22 January, 2004. <http://www3.aaos.org/research/imca/OAHip_Overview.htm>

_____. "Online Fact Sheet: Stress Fractures." 19 December, 2003. <http://orthoinfo.aaos.org/fact/thr_report.cfm?Thread_ID=46&topcategory=Sports&searentry=stress%20fractures>

_____. "Public Education and Media Relations." 30 November, 2003. <http://www6.aaos.org/pemr/press_release.cfm?PRNumber=82>

The American Dental Association and the American Academy of Orthopaedic Surgeons. "Antibiotic Prophylaxis for Dental Patients with Total Joint Replacements." Pamphlet. Updated 5 May, 2001.

American Red Cross. "Blood Banking Community Issues National Appeal for Immediate Donations." 20 April, 2004. <http://www.redcross.org/pressRelease/0%2C1077%2C0_314_2164%2C00.html>

Annals of Rheumatic Diseases Online. "Extreme Variations in Racial Rates of Total Hip Arthroplasty for Primary Coxarthrosis: A Population-Based Study in San Francisco." 14 December, 2003. <http://ard.bmjjournals.com/cgi/content/abstract/54/2/107>

Arthritis Foundation Home Page. "Osteoarthritis." 20 November, 2003. <http://www.arthritis.org/conditions/DiseaseCenter/oa.asp>

_____. "Rheumatoid Arthritis." 20 November, 2003. <http://www.arthritis.org/conditions/DiseaseCenter/ra.asp>

The Arthritis Society. "Canadians with Lower Income and Education Levels Have Limited Access to Joint Replacement Surgery, Research Shows." 20 November, 2003. <http://www.arthritis.ca/types%20of%20arthritis/default.asp?s=1>

_____. "Introduction to Arthritis." 11 January, 2004. <http://www.arthritis.ca/toolbox/headline%20news/news%20releases/osteo/default.asp?s=1>

Azom.Com. "Porous Coatings for Improved Implant Life." 22 December, 2003. <http://www.azom.com/details.asp?ArticleID=1900>

Betterhumans News. "Joints Built from Stem Cells." 20 December, 2003. <http://www.betterhumans.com/News/news.aspx?articleID=2003-12-01-8>

Biopharma.montreal.com. "Biosyntech: Successful Cartilage Regeneration." 20 December, 2003. <http://www.biopharma-montreal.com/biopharma/newsshownews.jsp?pNewsID=1104>

Biosyntech. "Cartilage Repair Is Now a Reality." 20 December, 2003. <http://www.biosyntech.com/en/NEWS42.htm>

_____. "Clinical Update on Biosyntech's Cartilage Repair Device, BST-CarGel." 20 December, 2003. <http://www.biosyntech.com/en/news40.htm>

Canadian Blood Services. "Blood Safety & the Security of Canada's Blood System." 22 March, 2004. <http://www.bloodservices.ca/CentreApps/Internet/UW_V502_MainEngine.nsf/page/E_FAQSafety_Security!OpenDocument>

_____. "Roll up your Sleeves, Canada." 22 March, 2004. <http://www.bloodservicesca/CentreApps/Internet/UW_V502_MainEngine.nsf/web/8290749958CD985385256AF6006686CC?OpenDocument>

Cafepress.Com. Totally Hip Shop. 12 March, 2004. <http://www.cafeshops.com/totallyhipshop>

Canadian Orthopaedic Foundation. "Clinical Realities: Too Few Surgeons, Too Many Patients." (Condensed from "Canada in Motion.") 28 November, 2003. <http://www.canorth.org/clinrealities.htm>

Charnley, G.J., M.D. "Hip Replacement: The Facts 2002." 24 November, 2003. <http://www.essexhipsurgeon.co.uk/hip_replacement_surgery.html>

C-Health.Com. "Canadians Waiting Months to over a Year for Joint Replacements." 11 January, 2004. <http://www.canoe.ca/Health0105/24_surgery-cp.html>

Children's Hospital of Pittsburgh. "Ice Hockey." 18 December, 2003. <http://www.chp.edu/besafe/adults/02hockey>

Click 10.Com. "Ceramic Hip Operation Offers Superior Performance, Doctor Says." 23 December, 2003. <http://www.click10.com/health/2609832/detail.html>

Corin Group. "Frequently Asked Questions." 31 December, 2003. <http://www.resurfacingofthehip.com/resurfacing7.htm>

_____. "The Implant." 31 December, 2003. <http://www.resurfacingofthehip.com/resurfacing3.htm>

_____. "A Patient's Guide to Hip Resurfacing." 31 December, 2003. <http://www.resurfacingofthehip.com/>

Fortune Archives. "Why HMOs Aren't the Future of Health Care." 26 January, 2003. <http://www.bebeyond.com/KeepCurrent/Indepth/Articles/HMO-future.htm>

The Fraser Institute. "Waiting Your Turn. Hospital Waiting Lists in Canada (13th Edition.)" 7 May, 2004. <http://www.fraserinstitute.ca/shared/readmore.asp?sNav=pb&id=587>

Gabriel, Peggy. *"Hip Replacement or Hip Resurfacing: A Story of Choices."* Bloomington, Indiana: 1stBooks Library, 2003.

Grelsamer, Ronald P., M.D. *What Your Doctor May Not Tell You about Hip and Knee Replacement Surgery: Everything You Need to Know to Make the Right Decisions.* New York: Warner Books, 2004.

Gillespie, Bonnie. "National Volunteer Donor Month Combats Blood Shortages." <u>The American Red Cross</u>. 16 April, 2004. <http://www.redcross.org/article/0,1072,0_497_2144,00.html>

The Guidant Europe Cardiovascular Institute. "Focus on Osteo-porosis: a Healthcare Priority in the European Union." 23 January, 2004. <http://www.eucomed.be/docs/MT-IP-hip%20replacement.pdf>

Harborview Injury and Prevention Research Center. University of Washington. "Recreational Injury Interventions: Ice Hockey." 22 December, 2003. <http://depts.washington.edu/hiprc/childinjury/topic/recreation/icehockey.htm>

Health Canada.com. "Health Canada — Warnings — Advisories. Voluntary Recall of Some Ceramic Hip Replacements." 18 December, 2003. <http://www.hc-sc.gc.ca/english/protection/warnings/2001/2001_101e.htm>

Hip and Knee Clinic of Newark, Delaware. "Hip Replacement Information." 1 January, 2004. <http://www.hipreplacement.medical-assessment.com/>

Hip Replacement Surgery Resource Directory. "Complete Patient Resource." 1 October, 2003. <http://www.hip-replacement-surgery.com/>

Huddleston, Herbert D., M.D. "Sir John Charnley." 14 November, 2003. <http://www.hipsandknees.com/hip/charnley.htm>

Jeffries, Lillian. "Patient with Debilitating Pain Treated with the Urgency of a Common Cold." The Foundation for Taxpayer & Consumer Rights. 18 January, 2004. <http://www.consumerwatchdog.org/healthcare/st/st000336.php3>

Joint Replacement Center. "Can a Total Hip Replacement Truly Last a Lifetime?" 24 December, 2003. <http://www.celebrationjointreplacement.com/lifetime.htm>

_____. "Guide to Hips." 24 December, 2003. <http://www.celebrationjointreplacement.com/hips.htm>

Joint Replacement Resource Center. "Should I Have a Joint Replacement?" 19 December, 2003. <http://my.webmd.com/content/article/57/66162.htm?rdserver=www.jointswebmd.com/>

Kalas, William and Jannarone, Thomas. "Alcoholic Beverage Control for Nightclub, Bar and Restaurant Owners." 10 December, 2003. <http://www.nightclublawyer.com>

Kids Health Organization. "Preventing Children's Sports Injuries." 18 December, 2003. <http://kidshealth.org/parent/firstaid_safe/outdoor/sports_safety_p2.htm>

Klapper, Robert, and Huey, Lynda. *Heal Your Hips: How to Prevent Hip Surgery — and What to Do if You Need It.* New York: John Wiley & Sons, 1999.

Law Dudes.com. "Liquor Licensee Information on Dram Shop, Liquor Liability." 10 December, 2003. <http://lawdudes.com/dramshop.htm>

Looksmart. "Geriatrics: Men at Increased Risk for Death Following Hip Fracture." 20 December, 2003. <http://www.findarticles.com/cf_dls/m2578/12_55/6816 3677/p1/article.jhtml>

_____. "National Blood Shortage Becoming Critical in United States." AORN Online. (Association of periOperative Registered Nurses.) 5 February, 2004. <http://www.findarticles.com/cf_dls/m0FSL/3_72/65539092/p1/article.jhtml>

Lubkin, Thelma. "Notes on My Total Hip Replacement." 23 August, 2003. <http://www.armory.com/~mom/THR.html>

Marshfield Clinic Cattails. "Total Ceramic Hip Replacement Now Available." 28 December, 2003. <http://www.marshfieldclinic.org/cattails/03/mayjun/defaultasp?artID=5>

May-Bowser, Linda. "Celebrities." Totally Hip Support Group. 20 November, 2003. <http://members.tripod.com/totallyhip1/educate/celebrities.htm>

_____. "Eddie Van Halen Gets Hip – Literally." 20 November, 2003. <http://members.tripod.com/totallyhip1/educate/celebrities.htm>

_____. "Sex after THR: Sexual Activity Guidelines following Total Hip Replacement Surgery." 12 March, 2004. <http://members.tripod.com/totallyhip1/educate/sexthr.htm>

Mayo Clinic.org. "Mayo Clinic Study Finds Total Hip Replacement among Patients Age 90 and Older Provides Better Quality of Life for Years After." 15 December, 2003. <http://www.mayoclinic.org/news2003-rst/1691.html>

McCullen, Geoffrey, M.D. and Miller, Ryle, Jr. *Hip and Knee Replacement: A Patient's Guide.* New York: W.W. Norton & Company, 1996.

McMahon, Stephen. "Total Hip Replacement." Stephen McMahon's Orthopaedics Web Site. 15 December, 2003. <http://www.joint-replacements.com/>

Mechanical Engineering Department. The University of Texas at Austin. "The Results of Total Hip Replacements." 15 December, 2003. <http://www.me.utexas.edu/~uer/hips/>

Microsoft® Encarta® Online Encyclopedia 2003. "Arthritis." 13 November, 2003. <http://encarta.msn.com © 1997-2003 Microsoft Corporation>

Mothers Against Drunk Drivers Online. "Don't Call Me Lucky." 10 December, 2003. <http://www.madd.org/stats/0,1056,1112,00.html>

_____. "Law Enforcement Fact Sheet." 10 December, 2003. <http://www.madd.org/ stats/0,1056,6751,00.html>

_____. "Statistics." 10 December, 2003. <http://www.madd.org/victims/0,1056,1899, 00.html>

National Institute of Arthritis and Musculoskeletal and Skin Diseases. "Questions and Answers about Avascular Necrosis." 15 December, 2003. <http://www.niams.nih.gov/hi/topics/hip/hiprepqa.htm>

_____. "Questions and Answers about Hip Replacement." 10 December, 2003. <http://www.niams.nih.gov/hi/topics/avascular_necrosis/>

National Institute of Health Consensus Statements 98. "Total Hip Replacement." 17 December, 2003. <http://consensus.nih.gov/cons/098/098_statement.htm#7_What0_Ar>

New Jersey Drunk Driving Lawyers. "National and State Drunk Driving Laws." 10 December, 2003. <http://www.newjerseydrunkdrivinglawyers.com/NationalandStateDrunkDrivingLaws>

New Jersey DWI.com. "New Jersey Drunk Driving DWI Information." 1 January, 2004. <http://www.newjerseydwi.com/>

Newtown Hadassah Newsletter. "Did You Know? What's Going on in the World of Hadassah?" 17 December, 2003. <http://home.comcast.net/~NewtownHadassah/diduknow.htm#Newsletter>

New York Post. "The Cost of Drunk Driving Even if You Do Not Drive a Car." 26 December, 1985.

Orthogate.com. "A Patient's Guide to Artificial Hip Replacement." 4 November, 2003. <http://www.orthogate.com/modules.php.?op=modload&name=Subjects&file=index&req=viewpage&pageid=1>

Orthopedic Institute at Memorial Medical, Springfield, Illinois. "Total Hip Replacement Surgery." 6 December, 2003. <http://www.memorialmedical.com/services/hip-replacement.htm>

Osteonics. "How Long Will the Joint Replacement Last?" 15 December, 2003. <http://www.howost.com/patientinformation/treatmentoptions/replacementlast.php>

_____. "What Are the Risks of Joint Replacement Surgery?" 15 December, 2003. <http://www.howost.com/patientinformation/treatmentoptions/surgeryrisks.php>

_____. "What Things Can't I Do After Joint Surgery?" 15 December, 2003. <http://www.howost.com/patientinformation/treatmentoptions/cantaftersurgery.php>

The Paget Foundation — for Paget's Disease of Bone and Related Disorders. "Information for Patients; Paget's Disease of Bone." 15 November, 2003. <http://www.paget's.org/>

PBS Home. "Medicare HMOs." 26 January, 2004. <http://www.pbs.org/healthweek/featurep1_513.htm>

Premier Healthcare Resource, Inc. "What Will Become of the HMO?" 24 January, 2004. <http://www.premierhealthcare.com/cgi-bin/article.cgi?article_id=567>

Pryor, Sally R. *Getting Back on Your Feet: How to Recover Mobility and Fitness After Injury or Surgery to Your Foot, Leg, Hip or Knee.* Post Mills, Vermont: Chelsea Green Publishing Company, 1991.

Rogers, Carolyn. "National Joint Registry Explored: Moving Ahead with Pilot Project; Legislation to Be Considered." 23 March, 2004. AAOS-Online. <http://www.aaos.org/wordhtml/bulletin/feb02/fline1.htm>

Rose, Eric A. M.D. *Second Opinion: the Columbia Presbyterian Guide to Surgery.* New York: St. Martin's Press, 2000.

Silber, Irwin. *A Patient's Guide to Knee and Hip Replacement: Everything You Need to Know.* New York: Simon & Schuster, 1999.

Simon, M. T. *Hip Replacements: What You Need to Know.* Huntington, New York: Kroshka Books, 2000.

Sirois, Fuschia M., and Gick, Mary L. "An Investigation of the Health Beliefs and Motivations of Complementary Medicine Clients." Journal of Social Science & Medicine, 2002.

Sirois, Fuschia M., and Gick, Mary L. "Treatment Seeking and Experience with Complementary/Alternative Medicine: A Continuum of Choice." The Journal of Alternative and Complementary Medicine, Volume 8, No. 2, 2002.

60 Minutes. "Your Shout/Your Fault." Willoughby, New South Wales: The Nine Network Australia. 20 May, 1986.

Smith & Nephew. "Compression Hip Screws Systems." 8 December, 2003. <http://ortho.smith-nephew.com/nl/Category. asp?NodeId=345>

Spine-health.com. "Bone Spurs (Osteophytes) and Back Pain." 10 January, 2004. <http://www.spine-health.com/topics/cd/spurs/ spurs01.html>

Stafinski, Tania and Menon, Dev. "The Burden of Osteoarthritis in Canada: A Review of Current Literature." (Working Paper 01-03) 28 November, 2003. <www.ihe.ca/publications/papers/ pdf/2001-03summary.doc>

Stassen, Joanne. "Blood Supply Could Run Dry by 2005." Capital News Online - a Publication of Carleton University's School of Journalism. 5 February, 2004. <http://temagami.carleton.ca/ jmc/cnews/29112002/feature.shtml>

Stem Cell Research Foundation. "Researchers Create Tissue-Engineered Joint from Stem Cells." 17 December, 2003. <http://www.stemcell researchfoundation.org/WhatsNew/December_2003.htm#1>

Stop Smoking Support. "How Smoking Destroys Blood Circulation." 12 December, 2003. <http://www.stopsmokingsupport.com/ blood.htm>

Stuttaford, Thomas, M.D. "A New Way to Replace the Hip." Thunder Ball Hip. 31 December, 2003. <http://www. thunderballhip.50megs.com/custom3.html>

Toronto Rehab. "Osteoarthritis Rehabilitation." 11 January, 2004. <http://www.torontorehab.on.ca/documents/Osteoarthritis.pdf>

Trahair, Richard. *All about Hip Replacement: a Patient's Guide.* New York: Oxford University Press, 1998.

20/20. "It's Not My Fault." New York: ABC News. 26 December, 1985.

University of Pennsylvania Orthopedic Journal. "Concepts of the Modern Ceramic on Ceramic Total Hip Arthroplasty and Early Results." 24 December, 2003. <http://www.uphs.upenn.edu/ortho/oj/2001/html/oj14sp01p1.html>

The University of Texas Southwestern Medical Center at Dallas. Department of Pathology. "Normal Reference Range Table." 22 January, 2004. <http://pathcuric1.swmed.edu/PathDemo/nrrt.htm>

University of Washington: Orthopedics & Sports Medicine. "What is Hip Replacement? A Review of Total Hip Arthroplasty, Hip Resurfacing, and Minimally-Invasive Hip Surgery." Edited by Seth S. Leopold, M.D. 24 December, 2003. <http://www.orthop.washington.edu/faculty/Leopold/hipreplacement/01>

The Utah Hip and Knee Center. "History of Total Joint Replacement." 28 November, 2003. <http://www.utahhipandknee.com/history.htm>

Villar, Richard. *Hip Replacement: a Patient's Guide to Surgery and Recovery.* San Francisco: Thorson's Publishing, 1995.

Virtual Hospital Orthopaedics. "Total Hip Replacement: A Guide for Patients." 1 December, 2003. <http://www.vh.org/adult/patient/orthopaedics/hipreplace/>

Warner, Chris. "Americans Want Cadillac Medicine at Chevrolet Prices." Panther Enterprises. 18 January, 2004. <http://www.seanet.com/~panther/>

Welch, Victoria. "Hip to Run." The Burlington Free Press. Burlington, Vermont. 22 January, 2004.

Wilcox, Melynda Dovel. "The Doctor is in Now." Kiplinger's Personal Finance Magazine. 18 January, 2004. <http://www.findarticles. com/cf_dls/m1318/2_54/58617163/p1/article.jhtml>

Women Fitness Canada Edition. "Research Finds Women Are More Proactive Than Men in Managing Their Health." 6 January, 2004. <http://www.womenfitness.net/ca_women_health.htm>

Wright.Com. "Orthopaedic Products, Biologic Implants, Knee, Hip and Shoulder Implants: Hip-Resurfacing." 25 December, 2003. <http://www.wmt.com/Patients/hip/resurfacing.asp>

Zimmer.Com. "Extending Hip Implant Life is the Goal." 1 December, 2003. <http://www.zimmer.com/ctl?op=global&action=1&id=25 61&template= PC#today>

_____. "Hip Implants Available Today." 1 December, 2003. <http://www.zimmer.com/ctl?op=global&action=1&id=2561&te mplate=PC>

_____. "Hip Replacement and Alternative Bearing Surfaces." 1 December, 2003. <http://www.zimmer.com/ctl?op=global&actio n=1&id=2561& template=PC#extending>

ELECTRONIC RESOURCES

Internet Support Groups

Totally Hip: a Free Online Support Group. <http://members.tripod.com/totallyhip1/> A comprehensive collection of articles, newsletters, personal stories, and illustrations of total hip replacements, as well as a warm and friendly discussion group.

Surfacehippy. This support group allows patients who have had hip resurfacing surgery to share information and experiences with each other. <http://health.groups.yahoo.com/group/surfacehippy/>

Yahoo! Total Joint Replacement. <http://health.groups.yahoo.com/group/Total_Joint_Replacement/> This helpful group answers questions about all kinds of joint replacements and has a physical therapist onboard.

Internet Web sites

Active Joints.com. <http://www.activejoints.com/> Describes hip resurfacing and a variety of hip replacement implants. Also discusses ways to preserve the joint and life after surgery from a patient's perspective.

Arthritis Insight.Com. <http://arthritisinsight.com/feature/replacements/links.html> Supplies numerous links to informative web sites on hip and knee replacements, and has a lively discussion board.

The Hip Doc.com. <http://thehipdoc.com> Presents educational information related to hip surgery, hip disease, and total hip replacements.

Hip Replacement.co.uk. <http://www.hipreplacement.co.uk> Provides a wealth of information about hip replacement surgery, its pros and cons, and what to expect before, during and after the operation.

Total Hip Replacement. <http://www.totalhipreplacement.net/index_ frames.htm> Offers information on hip replacement surgery, such as preoperative causes and treatment, surgical techniques and materials.

About the Author

Sigrid Macdonald is a freelance writer. Originally from New Jersey, Macdonald currently resides in Ottawa, Ontario. The Globe and Mail newspaper, The Women's Freedom Network and The Anxiety Disorders Association of Ontario have published her articles.

Printed in the United States
26062LVS00003B/249